GREENHOUSE GARDENING

The Essential Guide to Learn Everything About Greenhouses and How to Easily DIY to Produce Homegrown Fresh and Healthy Vegetables, Herbs, and Fruits

Mark Bennett

© Copyright 2020 by Mark Bennett. All right reserved.

The work contained herein has been produced with the intent to provide relevant knowledge and information on the topic on the topic described in the title for entertainment purposes only. While the author has gone to every extent to furnish up to date and true information, no claims can be made as to its accuracy or validity as the author has made no claims to be an expert on this topic. Notwithstanding, the reader is asked to do their own research and consult any subject matter experts they deem necessary to ensure the quality and accuracy of the material presented herein.

This statement is legally binding as deemed by the Committee of Publishers Association and the American Bar Association for the territory of the United States. Other jurisdictions may apply their own legal statutes. Any reproduction, transmission, or copying of this material contained in this work without the express written consent of the copyright holder shall be deemed as a copyright violation as per the current legislation in force on the date of publishing and subsequent time thereafter. All additional works derived from this material may be claimed by the holder of this copyright.

The data, depictions, events, descriptions, and all other information forthwith are considered to be true, fair and accurate unless the work is expressly described as a work of fiction. Regardless of the nature of this work, the Publisher is exempt from any responsibility of actions taken by the reader in conjunction with this work. The Publisher acknowledges that the reader acts of their own accord and releases the author and Publisher of any responsibility for the observance of tips, advice, counsel, strategies and techniques that may be offered in this volume.

Table of Contents

Introduction 7

PART I - THE IMPORTANCE OF GREENHOUSES 9

Chapter 1: The History of Greenhouses 10
    Glass Roofs 11
    Today's Greenhouses 12

Chapter 2: Advantages and Disadvantages 13

Chapter 3: The Differences 15
    Cultivation 15
    Cost Vs. Product Quality 16

PART II - BUILDING A GREENHOUSE 19

Chapter 4: Greenhouse Types 20
    Attached 20
    Windowfarm 21
    Freestanding Greenhouses 21
    Mini Greenhouses, Hotbed, and Cold Frame 27
    Figuring Out Your Greenhouse Design Depending on Your Climate 28
    Materials 29
    Why Do You Need a Certain Design for a Certain Climate 29
    Types of Climates and the Greenhouses for Them 30
    Structural Designs 34
    Backyard Greenhouses 35

Chapter 5: Lean-To Greenhouse 36

Chapter 6: Hoop House **39**

Chapter 7: Multi-Span Greenhouse **43**

Chapter 8: A-Frame Greenhouse **48**

Chapter 9: Post and Rafter **53**

Chapter 10: Keeping Your Greenhouse Running **59**

    What Plants to Grow 59

    Light Transmission... 61

    Controlling the Environment... 63

    CO2 63

    Watering Your Plants 64

    Propagation 64

    Misting.. 64

Chapter 11: Tips and Tricks **66**

    Starting Seeds Seasonally... 66

    Thermometers.. 67

    Lights 67

    Keep Your Greenhouse Tidy 67

    Heating.. 68

    How Much Space Do Your Plants Need 68

    Cooling.. 68

    Begin With Seeds Instead of Cuttings or Seedlings 69

    Ventilation.. 69

    Grow Things That Need to Be Grown Inside a Greenhouse 70

Chapter 12: Myths About Greenhouse Gardening............ **71**

Chapter 13: Mistakes Made By Beginner Gardeners........ **75**

PART III - PRODUCING PRODUCE YEAR-ROUND 81

Chapter 14: What to Grow 82

    Best Vegetables for a Greenhouse... 82

    Best Herbs for a Greenhouse 87

    Best Fruits for a Greenhouse... 90

Chapter 15: Plant Schedules 93

    Growing Guide and Planting Schedule......................................94

Chapter 16: Caring for Your Plants.................................. 101

    Starting Seeds... 101

    Pollination 101

    Crop Steering...102

    Pruning and Trellising..103

    Fertilizing 105

    Pests 106

Chapter 17: Dealing With the Seasons 108

    Year-Round Growing..108

Chapter 18: Flowers and Ornamentals 113

Chapter 19: How Greenhouses Affect Life 117

Chapter 20: Is a Greenhouse Business Really Profitable 121

Conclusion 123

BONUS

To get the

"*How to Clean and Disinfect your Greenhouse*"

Guide for Free,

use this link and you will receive it immediately:

http://bit.ly/CleanDisinfectyourGreenhouse

Enjoy the Reading!

Introduction

Congratulations on purchasing this book, and thank you for doing so. I hope that you find the information helpful and informative as you start your greenhouse adventure.

The following chapters will discuss the various aspects of greenhouses and greenhouse gardening and how you can create your own. Many people have decided to start gardening simply because it is fun and gives them access to fresh produce. The downside to regular gardening is that you will only have crops during the year's warm parts. Well, with greenhouse gardening, that's no longer a problem. You can produce amazing fruits and vegetables all year round. This book is here to show you how to do just that.

The book is separated into three main sections. In the first section, we will go over the history of greenhouses, as well as the advantages and disadvantages of having a greenhouse. We will also look at the differences between regular gardening and greenhouse gardening.

The second section is where the bulk of the information is. It is here that you will learn about the different types of greenhouses and how to pick the right greenhouse for you. We'll also go over how to build five different greenhouses on your own and the basic cost of doing so. You'll also find information on how to keep your greenhouse running efficiently and all of the tools you will need. We'll also go over some essential tips and common mistakes that you should avoid.

In the last section, we will talk about growing your crops. We'll discuss the best things to grow in your greenhouse, as well as the best planting schedule to go by so that you have something growing all year. We'll also go through the most important things like caring for your plants, avoiding pests and disease, and fertilizing them. We'll also go over how the season changes can affect your greenhouse. Then we learn how to grow flowers and ornamental plants in the greenhouse as well. Lastly, we'll look at how greenhouse gardening can affect your life.

As you can see, we've got a lot of information to cover, so let's get started. Please enjoy!

PART I

THE IMPORTANCE OF GREENHOUSES

*Thanks for choosing this book,
let's start the journey!*

*Make sure to leave a review on Amazon
if you like it, I'd really love to hear your thoughts!*

Chapter 1: The History of Greenhouses

The first greenhouses were built many centuries ago when the Romans created what we now call a "modern lifestyle." They didn't like going without fresh produce just because it wasn't their growing season. They wanted to find a solution to this problem, so they figured out how they could grow plants inside and invented the greenhouse.

The first known record of greenhouses was in Rome from about 30 AD. The legend states that Emperor Tiberius's physicians had told him he needed to eat one cucumber every day for his health. Thus, the engineers and scientists in Rome started brainstorming about ways to grow plants all year long. They didn't want to disappoint their emperor, so they created a cart that they planted cucumbers in that could be rolled outside to get sun during the day but could be brought inside on colder days.

During the 13th century in Italy, they built the first true greenhouse. It was called "the botanical garden." It was used to protect the tropical plants that the explorers brought home from exotic places. These early gardeners figured out ways to adjust their methods so that the sun's natural movements could be used to make sure the plants got the most warmth and sunlight.

This idea of having a special space where trees and plants could be protected, and they could grow no matter what the time of year it was or the climate was very attracted and it soon spread throughout Europe. The Netherlands started building them first, and it soon moved into England and on to France.

These early greenhouses became playgrounds for the rich, and they used them to grow their favorite flowers and fruits. The Royal Family of France loved oranges, so they grew evergreen orange trees in Versailles' garden. They would move the trees during winter from the outside gardens into the heated structures that had been made with a wooden frame, stonewalls, and a solid roof. These structures soon became known as "orangeries."

Greenhouses finally made it to America in the 1700s. In 1737, a Boston merchant, Andrew Faneuil, built the first greenhouse in America. George Washington wanted to serve his guests' fresh pineapple, so he had a greenhouse built at his home located at Mt. Vernon. He called his greenhouse "the Pinery." Just like in England, American greenhouses became more affordable and famous during the 19th century.

Glass Roofs

During the 15th century, the glassmakers in Murano, Italy that was located near Venice, figured out a way to make transparent glass. This was soon used to make glass roofs for the early greenhouses and orangeries. This invention completely changed greenhouses' history. They were soon renamed either conservatories or glasshouses.

Until about the 19th century, these greenhouses were only for the powerful and wealthy and would be built for the lady of the house so she could enjoy orchids and roses all year long. Most of the famous castles had elaborate, huge conservatories that were full of exotic trees and plants.

Today's Greenhouses

Greenhouses today are a lot different from those Roman cucumber carts. They are becoming more and more automated, which lets people save time on watering and other greenhouse chores. Greenhouses can have automatic misters that control the humidity and temperature, vents that automatically close and open depending on what temperature it is inside, a watering system that is automatic that will give the plants fertilizer and water when they need it, and heaters and fans that are also automatic. New materials such as polycarbonate, acrylic, and fiberglass panels are being used to make greenhouses even cheaper and more efficient.

The main thing that hasn't changed over the years is the passion for gardening. Just like it was during Roman times, gardeners today spend all their available moments taking care of the seedlings, fruits, vegetables, and flowers while experimenting to find better ways to improve them. If you have a greenhouse, you owe a lot to those ancient Roman cucumber carts.

As you can see, greenhouses have become very popular. Even though they were started as a way to meet royalty's nutritional needs, people also used them to grow medicinal plants so they would be readily available all year long. The science behind greenhouses has expanded, and universities now use them to further their research and studies. With all the advances within the agricultural industry, using greenhouses can be used by anyone.

Anyone who desires to begin their own business could incorporate the use of a greenhouse into their lives. If you would like to create your own greenhouse and grow your own flowers and produce, make sure you research and plan every single thing. You need to also know about the disadvantages and advantages of growing plants inside a greenhouse.

Chapter 2: Advantages and Disadvantages

Greenhouses are very popular, especially among those who want to have things growing all year long, but they come with disadvantages as well. It's important to understand the possible downsides to having a greenhouse. This will help you to come to the best decision for you.

Disadvantages

- **Lack of Pollination**

Even if you think you have the best control over your plants inside your greenhouse, some plants will carry pests like whiteflies that could quickly spread to all your other plants. This could sabotage most of your vegetables and plants you are growing. You also need to realize that natural pollinators aren't going to be able to get to your crops. This might be a huge disadvantage for some of the fruits and vegetables that you are growing.

- **Expensive to Operate**

In order to make sure your greenhouse is being used for its maximum output, you are going to need to invest in supplies that can make sure your crops have a great lifespan. If you install a cheap plastic film to keep heat in, it might be perfectly fine. But if you use more expensive glass windows, they will last longer, and you will be able to ventilate your greenhouse when you open them. When heating your greenhouse, you might notice a large increase in your monthly electric bills if you use heaters of any kind.

Advantages

- **Lowers Threats**

When you grow your plants inside a greenhouse, you can prevent predators from eating your crops. With a greenhouse, you are always in control of what comes in and out of your greenhouse. Plus, this kind of environment will protect your crops from disease, pests, and the weather. You can minimize the risks of insects and pests that could kill your plants.

- **Larger Variety**

When you get your produce at a grocery store or supermarket, you have to pay their price because they rely on production methods, availability, and demand. Different types of produce have various growing seasons. But, if you build your own greenhouse, you will have an opportunity to have a large variety of produce throughout the year. By doing this, you can create a more extensive assortment of products for consumers when markets have a lower supply. Greenhouses give you an opportunity to grow new vegetables or flowers that don't normally thrive where you live. Because of this, you might provide the best growing environment for whatever crop you decide to grow.

- **Extended Growing Season**

When you are creating your own greenhouse, your plants won't have to depend on the weather. Anybody would be delighted to know that they could grow any herb, fruit, or vegetable they want without having to worry about the weather. Any seed you decide to plant in your greenhouse will take root and grow even though they might not have under the best circumstances when grown outside.

The best advantage of having your own greenhouse is you can use various techniques to keep it at a constant temperature. By doing this, you will cause less stress on your plants. Plus, you will have more growth early in the growing season. One technique is known as thermal solar mass. To use this method, you will use natural materials that are able to absorb, store, and release thermal heat. You could also buy and use heating fans or other heaters.

Chapter 3: The Differences

These days farming can be challenging, with quality and quantity being more extensive than ever. Farmers need to keep up with the latest technology to produce better fruits and vegetables. This is going to require more expenses and implementing new methods.

Growing food in open fields has always been the most common way, but now it isn't your only option. You do risk losing your crops due to bad  weather, and this makes it harder to manage the weaker crops. This is the main reason farmers try to find other ways to grow their crops, and this is the main reason they choose to grow them in greenhouses. Let's look at the differences between growing crops in an open field and growing them in a greenhouse.

Cultivation

- **Greenhouse**

If you decide to grow your crops inside a greenhouse, you have more control over their environment. You can manage the light, humidity, irrigation, and temperature. You can use various methods of controlling all of these things, and you can protect your crops from being attacked by pests. When you have all the power over developing your crops, you are able to keep them healthier, and you will be able to predict the amount you will be harvesting.

How much it will cost you to set up a greenhouse might correspond with all the advantages your greenhouse can give you. If you grow your crops in a greenhouse, your yield might be ten to 12 times larger, making your crops more reliable than growing them in an open field. When you are able to control your growing environment, it can help you grow fruits, vegetables, flowers, or any other plant all year. Growing in a greenhouse can help you improve a plant's genetics, which means you will get a more substantial variety. You also won't need as much water inside a greenhouse as you do in an open field. You can't rely on insects to pollinate your crops. You are able to use still whatever pesticides or chemicals to keep your plants from getting diseases. You do have the bees for pollination in an open field, but you also risk losing your crops to insects or other animals.

- **Open Field**

Growing crops in an open field date back to the middle ages. When you use the land in this way, you need to make sure the soil is fertile, you have to sow the seeds or use seedlings, and then you have to protect them from all kinds of hazards until they are ready to harvest. Being out in the real world can be quite dangerous, like eroding soil, pest attacks, diseases, or fast climate changes. There is a lot you have to do to stay competitive in this market. Weather fluctuation is a lot more unpredictable now than it used to be. This means you will need to be prepared with the right way to react when faced with an emergency.

Just like anything else, it is going to take some effort. If you can grow healthy plants out in the open, your crops will be blessed with fresh air and sunlight that make them taste the best even though they might not all look the same.

Cost Vs. Product Quality

Growing your crops inside a greenhouse doesn't mean you aren't going to have good food. Plants that have been grown inside can be healthier since they aren't going to need as many pesticides and chemicals to survive. With all the latest technological advances, there isn't any difference in the taste of crops grown outside or inside.

As the demand continually grows for quality produce, it makes people have to constantly create new technologies and enhance their agriculture practices to be able to harvest more and more produce without losing any of its quality. When you have more control over the growing conditions, it enables you to have better yields, which will give you more profits and won't matter whether you grew them in a field or a greenhouse.

PART II

BUILDING A GREENHOUSE

Now we are about to go deeper into
Greenhouses Techniques

Chapter 4: Greenhouse Types

It is very important that you choose and build a greenhouse that is right for your property so that it can take advantage of the maximum amount of available sunlight. This all depends on selecting the proper greenhouse structure. I will be giving you a detailed description of all the greenhouse types out there and their disadvantages and advantages.

Before you choose a shape, you need to think about whether you want to build a freestanding or attached greenhouse. What are these, and how are they different?

Attached

Just like the name says, this kind of greenhouse will be attached to your house. One of the pros of having this type of greenhouse is you won't be using as many building materials as you would for a freestanding one.

The ventilation and heating tools could be used for your house, too. It does come with some drawbacks in terms of trying to control the temperature inside the greenhouse. The building that the greenhouse is attached to could shade the greenhouse and limit the amount of light that the plants need.

Attached greenhouses could be in two different shapes: even-span and lean-to.
A lean-to greenhouse is normally set up so that it is on the south-facing side of your house. The ridge of its roof will connect to the house. This kind of greenhouse is cheap and easy to heat, especially if you are in colder climates.

Even-span greenhouses will give you more space for more plants. How? The end wall will be attached to a house, and its rafters will be the same length. One con of this kind of greenhouse is the cost of the building and heating the inside as compared to the lean-to.

Because of this, you could just put the money into a freestanding greenhouse but don't forget that electricity and water can be reached easily when a greenhouse is attached to another building.
Basically, both an even-span and a lean-to attached greenhouse can have the same problems, and that is shadowing. The shadow of the building that the greenhouse is attached to will always cause a reduction in the amount of sunlight.

Windowfarm

This is an indoor, vertical garden that lets you grow plants in just about any window. It allows the plants to used natural sunlight. You will be using the same heating and cooling system as you do for your living space; all you need to do is add some organic liquid soil. This is a type of hydroponic farming.

This type of system is completely DIY. It is the best way for people to grow fresh produce, no matter where they live. You don't need a yard. The cheapest option is a starter kit that can be found online for under $200.

Since it is a hydroponic system, it will require more components like nutrients, tubes, and pumps and more maintenance than a normal soil-based greenhouse.

Freestanding Greenhouses

These are similar to the attached ones, and they can also be lean-to or even-span-shaped. Let's compare these two and move on to describe other types of freestanding ones.

- **Even-Span**

This type of greenhouse can be characterized by the rafters that are equally spaced, the roof trusses, and the building will support itself. There are many kinds available at most home improvement warehouses, or you can find them online. Most of these will allow you to choose between two types of coverings: 10mm polycarbonate or 3mm tempered glass.

This kind of structure can be easily recognized by the gable, which is a triangle between the sloped roof sides. This is the most common kind of greenhouse since it uses the most amount of sun.

It also has a lot of space inside that lets you grow various plants while keeping the optimal conditions. Even-span kinds usually require glass panels that run from the ground to the top and an aluminum frame for more support.

- **Uneven-Span**

This is the total opposite of the one above since the rafters will always be unequal, and it doesn't support itself. This is the best choice if you have a hill that you would like to use for something.

The best advantage of this kind of greenhouse is all the sunlight that it utilizes. The biggest disadvantage is the problems working inside because of the limited space and how it is configured.

- **Hoop House**

This can be easily identified by its curved roof or military-style hut design. These hoops are normally made from PVC or aluminum pipes and then covered with polyethylene panels or film to give it some insulation. Basically, this means that you will stretch a piece of plastic over a series of hoops. It could also be made using straight lines by using elbows for the PVC pipes to get the shape you want. This is the least expensive design of all the greenhouses. The construction would cost about one dollar per square foot.

The sidewalls will be very low, and this limits your headroom and storage space. This is the easiest and cheapest kind to build, and that is why most people like it. You can get it on most online shops for about $200 or even build one yourself.

A hoop house is useful because any type of precipitation will just roll off the roof easily. It is best for crops that grow low to the ground like strawberries or lettuce. You could use it to grow cucumbers and tomatoes.

Hoop houses aren't always cheap. If you love this shape and want to use the best type of materials, you can find them online. For a bit more money, you can get double-walled paneling that will last for ten years.

These are relatively easy to construct and can be adapted to small amounts of land. This shape is not as sturdy as an A-frame or the post and rafter.

- **Gothic Arch**

This kind of greenhouse is very aesthetically pleasing. This design can be easily identified by its walls being bent over to make a pointed roof that was inspired by the windows in Gothic cathedrals found around the world. It has a semicircular frame that is normally made from conduit or galvanized pipe. It is usually covered with plastic sheeting.

This kind of greenhouse is very wide and would be great for anybody who would like to grow their plants in rows. You can put plants on the shelves plus hang some pots inside as well. It is similar to the hoop house above and has the same functionally.

It conserves heat well. Its shape makes sure that snow will just slide off without accumulating on top. There are several different models to choose from, and make sure you research to find the one best for your climate.

The pros of this greenhouse are its efficient and simple design. Using plastic sheeting lowers the overall cost a lot. The design shape lets snow and water runoff easily.
It has some cons as the sidewalls' height is very low, which restricts the headroom and storage space.

- **A-Frame**

For me, this is the easiest and simplest greenhouse to set up, and it is charming. Its design allows you to save money on construction materials and is perfect for a tiny backyard.
All you have to do is to put short sidewalls and the roof together to form a triangular shape. The biggest problem that you might run into is the poor air circulation in its corners.

It is one of the more popular designs. The most significant advantage is its simple design and the fact that it doesn't use many materials. The typical coverings would be glass, but translucent, rigid polycarbonate panels can be used, and some kits come with this type of covering.

The pros of this kind of greenhouse are its simple design and the use of fewer materials. Some cons are its narrow sidewall that limits the functionality of using the whole greenhouse. Air circulation could be a problem in the corners.

- **Post and Rafter**

These are probably the most popular since most gardeners go for this kind. The construction is very simple and is the strongest out there. The structure is very practical, too. Because this design is a bit top-heavy, the frame needs to be footed. This will increase the cost as compared to the other designs.

This greenhouse uses heat and space very efficiently. With this greenhouse, you can cut down significantly on heat loss during the winter months. Again do some research online, and you might find one that you just have to have. Some designs even have a built-in gutter system so you can collect rainwater runoff if it is allowed in your area.

Its rafters give the roof more support during the winter months, but it might make the entire construction heavier, and this will require a stronger frame that might cost more. If you do decide on this type of greenhouse, make sure you create a foundation for it.

The most common covering options are normally glass, but rigid translucent polycarbonate panels can make the cost a lot lower. Its pros are its simple design, maximum space usage along the walls. It has better air circulation, especially along the walls. It does require more materials like metal and wood than other designs.

- **Mini Portable**

These are just like their name says... they are portable and small. They aren't large enough for you to get inside and are covered simply. They usually have some shelves to optimize the light and heat inside an enclosed outdoor area or inside your house.

Most of these are covered with plastic sheeting since they are portable and don't need to be excessively heavy. This keeps them lightweight and easily moveable if you need to.

Their small size makes them a good option for people who don't have a lot of floor space but want to have a greenhouse. They are easy to build and very affordable.

These greenhouses are not very sturdy and are too small for anyone who wants to be serious gardeners. You won't be able to grow too many plants in one of these small greenhouses.

- **Tabletop Greenhouse**

These are a simple DIY kind of greenhouse if you are very creative, and you don't have a lot of os pace in your home, but you want a safe place to keep and grow plants. They are very unique and pretty since you can make them from various materials and don't have one design. These can be made from old shadow boxes, picture frames, fish bowls, and a lot more. You could purchase some that have already been made.

These are normally made from panels of plastic, acrylic, or glass. The frames could be made from various materials depending on the look you want. They normally don't need covers other than what was mentioned bit if you put them in a cold space, you could use some plastic sheeting.

These treasures are affordable, compact, and used for decorative purposes, but they can absolutely keep a plant alive. With various DIY designs out there, you can have as many of these tiny treasures as you want.

Because they are very small, you are limited in the types of plants that you can put in them. If you don't build your own, most of the ones you can purchase don't come with any drainage, so these are best for plants that don't need a lot of water.
Since there are so many options out there and many DIY ideas for them, it might be hard to pick out just one. It all depends on how small or large you want your greenhouse to be, but your options are limitless.

Mini Greenhouses, Hotbed, and Cold Frame

All of these are basic greenhouses. The mini greenhouse that I am talking about shouldn't be confused with an actual mini greenhouse that is a small glazed professional or homemade house that can be short or tall and could either be horizontal or vertical.
A mini greenhouse is best used to start seeds. It can be as simple as a clear plastic container with a lid.

Cold frame greenhouses are ventilated boxes that are put on the ground with a sloping, glazed lid. It is best for raised beds during spring to help warm the soil. You can find these online for under $100. This is just a structure that covers your garden that will protect your plants from very low temperatures, rain, snow, and wind.

If you are doing this completely DIY, anything goes. You can use either plastic sheeting or glass. The one thing that is required is the covering needs to be able to be opened to ventilate the heat.

This is very popular because of its design. It is literally a box without a bottom that has a skylight. The cost is very reasonable, and many designs are made from scraps of wood and old windows.

The biggest disadvantage is overheating. A sunny afternoon with the window closed could cause some severe damage to the plants. Another disadvantage is the quality of the materials you are using. Old wood and glass are prone to being damaged and breaking.

A hotbed is a heated cold frame. The way you heat it will vary from electric cables, manure, steam, hot water, or light bulbs. You need to choose ones depending on what you will be growing.

What can you grow in these types of greenhouses? Well, to make it simple, a cold frame is best for plants that love the cold, like cauliflower, broccoli, and cabbage. If you want to grow plants that love heat, such as eggplants, tomatoes, and peppers, your best option would be a hotbed.

When you have finally made up your mind about the kind of structure you want, you can then begin thinking about coverings and the frame type.

Figuring Out Your Greenhouse Design Depending on Your Climate

Greenhouses are more than just protection for plants. It can help get the best from your plants and creates a productive, relaxing, and pleasant space. Having a tropical place to take refuge on cold days might seem ideal, but it takes a lot of research and planning to ensure that the right design for your climate has been chosen.

Your greenhouse could be airy, comfortable, green, and wonderfully lit, or it might be a plant's worst nightmare, which is a hot oven on a summer day or a freezer in the winter and dripping condensation everywhere all year long. The difference is your design.

Materials

Before 1950, greenhouses were thought of as a unit for only the wealthy who could hire personal gardeners to work in them to make sure their vegetables and fruits stayed productive all year long.

When inexpensive plastic sheeting was developed, it prompted a quick expansion of various kinds of greenhouses. Growers didn't have to worry about breakable glass panels and heavy components they need to support them.
This means that both people who like to garden as a hobby and professional growers had the same opportunities to buy or build their own greenhouses. These could be any design, shape, or size.

Once all the new plastic technology was developed, it sparked a quick expansion of a wide range of greenhouse kits available. Even though this sudden boom gave gardeners a large choice of protected structures that they could grow their plants in, they made some mistakes when choosing the right one for their climate.

Why Do You Need a Certain Design for a Certain Climate

All greenhouses aren't created equal. A design that works great in cooler climates that has long winters that are bitter cold with high winds, low sunlight, and lots of snow wouldn't be the best design for a tropical climate that is humid with various intensities of light.

All the different greenhouses get characterized by how much they protect plants from the environment outside so they can give the grower all the control they need for their certain conditions.

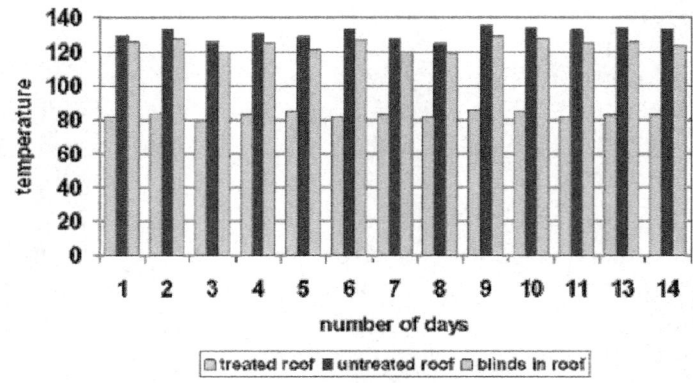

How much protection is needed all depends on the kind of plants you will be growing and your local climate. The main thing about building a greenhouse is to find the design that lets you overcome the most horrific climate problems in your area. This way you can get the best growth possible.

Types of Climates and the Greenhouses for Them

- **Desert or Dry, Tropical Climates**

In these kinds of climates, the temperatures can get extremely high, and I mean hot enough to kill most plants in a greenhouse unless you are growing cactus.
Temperatures that hit over 100 degrees all year long and combined with no humidity are normal for this kind of climate. The biggest threats are high winds that carry sand or dust that can blast both greenhouses and crops.

The best greenhouse for this extreme climate is a simple tent with some poles that have been set deeply into the ground made from high-tensile steel wires to create a frame that you will place a layer of fine insect mesh that has been stretched and secured.
This creates a shaded, insect-proof place that lets air flow adequately to keep the heat from building up. You can increase the humidity by misting or fogging inside, which will also

reduce the temperatures inside, usually to the level right below the one outside. Low humidity gives the environment the best use of evaporative cooling. This is the best feature for growing in this type of dry, hot climate.

Air movement is needed inside this greenhouse to keep good transpiration levels in the crop since this is another way to cool the plants naturally. More high-tech, computer-controlled structures that are air-conditioned can be used in these climates, too.

- **The Mediterranean and Subtropical Desert Climates**

Desert areas that are located in the latitudinal range of 30 to 35 degrees can have a lot lower temperatures during the winter, even though temperatures during summer are very high without much rainfall. To be able to produce crops year-round, most gardeners use hydroponics to grow their crops. This eliminates the need to dig into their hard dirt and ensure their plants stay adequately watered. Using a hydroponic garden inside of a greenhouse is a popular option for many. They need a structure that could be heated but still keeps the environment cool during summer.

For this kind of climate, the best structure would be a cooled plastic greenhouse with a heating system and vents along the top. A fan and pad system can increase humidity and cools the air—the humidity increases when the water evaporates inside the greenhouse. Along with shading the greenhouse, this can produce the best environment during hot and dry summer months.

When temperatures start dropping, which happens during the night, the moist air could be vented through the vents while the inside gets heated. This process can reduce humidity in the greenhouse to what it is outside, and this can prevent condensation from gathering when the temperatures get cooler outside.

Condensation is the biggest threat to crops grown in a greenhouse. When droplets of water fall onto the plants, it can create wetness on the leaves. This could cause bacteria and fungus to attack the plant, and this could cause an outbreak of diseases that are hard to control as new infections happen each night.

- **Tropical, Humid Climates**

Any tropical area will experience muggy and hot conditions during the night and day for most of the year. They get heavy downpours of rain regularly. In some lowland areas, the humidity can be unbearable. The levels of sunlight could fluctuate from being high on sunny days to being low during overcast days, especially during the rainy months.

Tropical areas that are located near the equator can experience short days. When you combine this with constant overcast conditions, it could reduce the amount of sunlight that is available for your crops. Insects are more populous in these tropical climates, and this requires you to put an insect mesh over the vents and any sides that open.

Some tropical gardeners choose to put their greenhouses in highland areas where temperatures are normally cooler and the humidity levels are better. A good greenhouse design for tropical areas could be as easy as a plastic roof or a rain cover that has sides that roll up or can open.

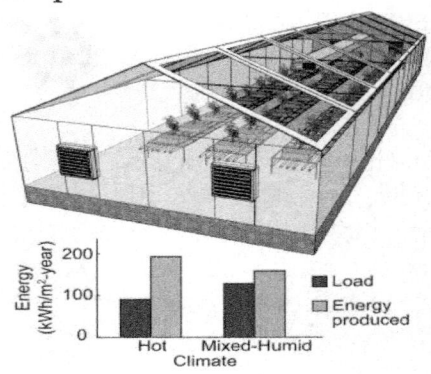

These will need to be covered with an insect mesh. In large greenhouses, this structure could be designed with a "sawtooth" roof that lets you vent the hot air out on days that are clear and hot.

The vent tops might feature a plastic cover that rolls up that will stretch down from the gutters to keep rain from getting into the greenhouse when it rains. Because temperatures are warm both day and night for most of the year, insulation and heating aren't needed. You can leave the vents open as long as an insect mesh covers them.

Fans that move air and misting systems could be used to cool the inside of the greenhouse. You could use thermal screens that you can move to reduce brightness or sunlight on days that are clear to allow the most light to get through the greenhouse.

Because high winds from hurricanes and typhoons are major risks in this type of climate, these greenhouses have been designed so the insect mesh covers can be moved from the building before they cause any framework damage.

- **Temperate Climates**

This type of climate can be found in most hydroponic systems. These get characterized by various seasonal temperatures and moderate rainfall throughout the year. This variance in temperatures is enough so that you might have to modify the environment for part of your growing season when the outdoor weather isn't suitable. Normally this will have to be done when the temperatures are too cold for plant growth. Heating the air inside the greenhouse effectively and then maintaining and insulating the heated air is the only thing you need to worry about.

Gardeners who want high growth rates all year and the most yields normally choose a greenhouse that features sidewalls that are completely clad with side and roof vents that allows for larger ventilation areas. You might need a computer to help you control the environment like vents, fogging, thermal screens, shades, or heaters.

Greenhouses in this zone normally use two plastic sheet layers, but the space between these layers gets inflated. This gives better insulation and better control of the environment.

- **Cold Climates**

Cold climates are any areas that are located above the latitude of 45 degrees. They can be characterized by the huge variation in the length of day and their temperatures, especially within the continental areas.

During the day, temperatures could hit below freezing for most of the years, and the days are very short. The coastal areas will have mild but short summers and longer days. Temperatures during the day in summer could be somewhat high in the central regions in Russia or Canada.

The best greenhouse for this environment needs to have solid walls that are constructed very strongly. They always need to have steep roofs that are sturdy to carry the snow that might cause plastic sheeting to collapse.

These greenhouses need to be double insulated by using plastic sheeting on the inside of the walls and placing movable thermal screens across the eaves at the height of the studs. In order to stop heat from being lost, vents need to be kept closed during the winter. This, along with the short days, means you will need to inject carbon dioxide into the greenhouse, and you will need to add lighting if you are using a hydroponic system.

Structural Designs

Most hydroponic greenhouses will have a height of about ten feet and sometimes higher. This is a lot higher than most of the earlier greenhouse designs that were very low to the ground so that you couldn't stand up inside.

It doesn't matter the design or type of greenhouse or what you plant on growing inside them; a taller greenhouse will give you the best environment for your plants and a bigger buffer against temperature changes.

The larger design gives you a better capacity for the movement of air that is needed to grow crops. The movement of air can benefit many crops by reducing diseases and improving transpiration.

The amount of air that is needed has to be heated if you are in a colder climate can be accomplished by putting thermal screens across the roof during the night. This helps hold the heat inside the greenhouse so the heat won't be wasted by escaping through the vents.

Backyard Greenhouses

For people who are serious about growing their crops using hydroponics and want the biggest harvests, their best option would be to build a smaller version of a large commercial greenhouse for their climate.

Some design faults you need to be aware of in some greenhouse kits would be that the structure is too small to restrict the airflow and cause the heat to buildup too fast.
Check to make sure it has a large top vent. The windows need to be able to be opened manually to vent the greenhouse. You could also install a roll top vent in the roof too. Stay away from any kit that relies on a small door that vents the greenhouse because this never works with warmer growing conditions.
You should only use plastic sheeting, which is the best quality. It needs to be UV stabilized and should last for three years. Make sure you can get replacement sheeting if needed.
Most hydroponic growers have come to love a very well-constructed greenhouse, but getting all the basics figured out before you begin construction is necessary for your crops' health and productivity.

Figuring out the kind of climate you live in, knowing the limiting factors that it imposes on your crops, and understanding the best kind of greenhouse that will help you overcome all these limitations is what you need to do before you begin anything.
These same principles about the design of greenhouses apply to both small backyard greenhouses and huge commercial structures. Getting the basics under your best during the construction will help your greenhouse be productive.

Chapter 5: Lean-To Greenhouse

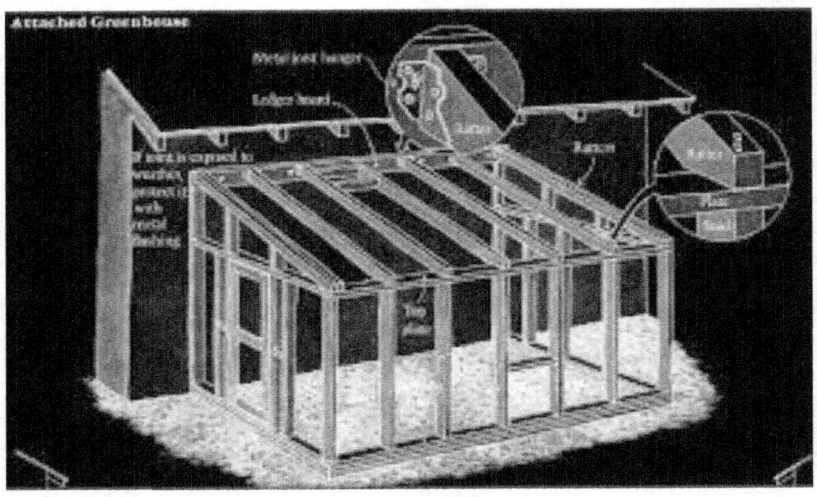

The first greenhouse we are going to learn how to build is the lean-to greenhouse. This is an excellent option if you have a wall available that is in a sunny location. You can even use a patio that you don't ever use. These types of greenhouses can be customized really quickly, and this particular one will look a bit different from others. Instead of opening at the ends, you would use existing windows or doors of your patio to use it. It is also built at waist height so that you don't have to bend over and hurt your back. This is going to be on the small side, so plan accordingly.

Materials

- 2x4s, 1x10 barn board siding, ¾" plywood, 1x2 battens
- Deck screws
- Roof screws with rubber washers
- Suntuf polycarbonate panels
- Old wood windows

Tools

- Drill
- Jigsaw
- Level and square
- Paint stripper (if needed)

Building The Greenhouse
Start out by taking off the wood on the outside wall if need be, and strip off any paint from old windows. You'll then caulk, prime, and paint them. You can then frame them into place on the wall. The main thing with framing them in is that they need to be snug so that you will have control over the temperature of your greenhouse. The windows will need to be attached with hinges and latches since this is your access to the greenhouse.

Then you will build the base of the greenhouse. Run a 2x4 underneath the windows that you just fixed. This will vary in length, depending on the size of your windows. At each end, attach a 4x4 that has been cut so that the top reaches just underneath the windows. Place a third 4x4 in the center. Cut the 1x10 so that you have a piece that is as long as the 2x4 you used earlier. Then cut two smaller pieces of the 1x10 to whatever width you would like your greenhouse. Attach one end of the shorter piece to the 4x4 and then attach another 4x4 to the other end. Do the same thing on the far end. Then attach the longer board to the 4x4s. Place another 4x4 in the middle of this board opposite the one under the windows.

Then cut a sheet of plywood to fit on top of the box you made. It should rest on top of the 4x4s.

Next, you will make the rafters for the roof. The space between the rafters will depend on the plastic sheets you have as the rafters need to be just a bit smaller than the panels. This goes best if you mock up your rafters as you go. You will need shorter pieces of the rafter, about 18" with one end up at a 60-degree angle. These will be spaces equal on top of the outside edge of your greenhouse. You will then need a longer piece of the rafter that reaches from the top of the small pieces to the side of your half. This is the part that you will need to play around with, as it will depend on how wide you made your greenhouse. You will also need to cut the ends, 60-degree angles. Attach these to the side of the house and the shorter rafters. Use triangle pieces of plywood as gussets on the rafter pieces. This will secure them more. Then go around the top of the box you made with 2x4 pieces place on their side to box things in a bit more. This will give shape to your greenhouse.

Next, you will use another piece of plywood, cut into a triangle, and close to the top of the greenhouse. Don't worry about closing in the entire end because you will be adding the panels.

Next, you will need to install your panels. These panels are really easy to install ad you will use those screws and washers to install them. Then you can set up the inside of the greenhouse however you would like.

Chapter 6: Hoop House

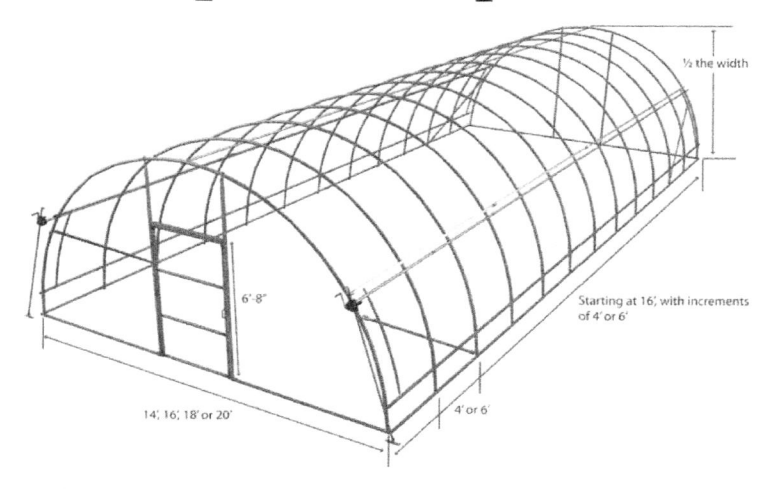

A hoop house greenhouse is a very common greenhouse to see as they are extremely easy to make and are cheaper to build than other greenhouses. Since these greenhouses are such a simple concept, a simple hoop-shaped structure made of metal or plastic framing and then covered with plastic, they make a great and inexpensive DIY project that allows for flexibility for experimentation.

This greenhouse will be 165 square feet, making it a pretty decent sized greenhouse with lots of space for growing plants. An easy way to grow plants in this greenhouse is to use two built-in plant beds that run along the sides of the greenhouse. You could also easily add in free-standing shelves for an additional place to plant and for starting seeds or to overwinter potted plants.

It is completely possible to create a greenhouse like this one on a budget. Depending on the types of things you do around your house, there is a good chance that you may already have a lot of the materials on hand. If you don't, there is a good chance that a search through Facebook or Craigslist would turn up some people trying to get rid of the things you need. And even if you had to go out and buy everything for this project, it would only run you around $200, which is a lot less than one of those kits for a similar-sized greenhouse.

You will need to have a level, flat, well-drained area for your hoop house, but it's also worth looking at how sheltered it is. Even moderate winds could exert a lot of force on this type of greenhouse, so choosing a spot with some shelter from tree cover or other buildings could be a good idea. Since excess heat can be an issue during the summer, try to orient the house to make sure the ends are pointed in directions that will allow for a lot of ventilation.

This is the own how-to that does not come with specifics because it can easily adjust to your needs. We will go over the basics of what you need to know to build the hoop house, and then you can make it yours.

Materials

- 2x6 treated wood
- Three-inch screws
- 35-inch long PVC ground pipes
- A 10-foot long and 20-foot long piece of PVC pipe for each hoop with a factory flared end
- Lock bolt
- Purlins
- UV-safe plastic

Tools

- Level and square
- Drill
- Circular saw
- Knife or scissors for cutting the plastic

Building The Greenhouse

No matter what size you are making your greenhouse, you will start by making a four-sided ground frame from treated wood. 2x6s set on their side will work for a house that ranges from 14 to 18-feet wide. If your hoop house is smaller than that, you should use 2x4s.

If you need longer sides than the pieces of wood that you have, just use a 24-inch batten to splice the joints together. Galvanized three-inch wood screws work best when splicing them together. To secure the corners, you should use four-inch screws. Set your frame where you want it, measure it, and then make sure the diagonal measurements are equal. Drive temporary stakes into the earth on the outside corners so that the frame does move out of square.

You will need some ground pipes for the next part. These are 36-inch-long PVC pounded into the ground. Drive one into each corner of the wooden frame, and then another at every three feet along the long sides. They should all be tight to the inside face of the ground frame. Each of these will support one hoop pipe. As you work, have somebody hold a scrap piece of wood on top of the stake as you hit it so that the PVC doesn't break. The pipes should be driven in flush with the top of the ground frame.

How long your hoop pipes need to be will depend on how wide your hoop house is. One ten-foot and one 20-foot length of pipe are needed for each hoop on an 18-foot-wide design. You will want to make sure you have a factory-flared end on each pair of pipes that come together to make the hoop. The flared end will slip over the straight end of the other piece. When you join the pipes, make sure that you use PVC cement to ensure they stay together.
The amount of arch you have in your hoop house can vary depending on how tall you would like it to be. If you have a narrower hoop house, you will want to get shorter pipes.

Layout the pipes where they are going to go. If you need to, get some help to raise them. First, slip one end of the pipe into its ground pipe, then bend your pipe so that it will fit into the ground pipe on the other side. Install all of these hoops as such, then drill a .5" hole for lock bolts through the wooden frame, hoop pipe, and the ground pipe for the lock bolt. Make sure that the hoop pipe has been pushed all of the ways down, and do it only one end for now. Place in a four-inch-long carriage bolt into each of these holes. You will then need to use a ladder so that you can sight along the tops of all of your hoops. You want the peaks to all be about the same height. This is why you left one end unbolted so you can adjust if need be.

Then you will need to add purlins. This secures the hoops even more. These are horizontal pipes that attach to the hoops for strength. You will need at least one purling installed along the ridge, with two others placed part way down each side. These pipes need to go on the inside of the hoops and be secured with a smooth head carriage bolt facing up.

Next, you will need to place it on the plastic. Choose a day when it isn't windy and unroll the UV-safe plastic. Leave around 12 inches of extra plastic at the edges and 24" on the ends. Wrap this excess around rubber balls every four to five feet. Tie the balls in place using ropes. Toss the other ends of the ropes over the peak of your hoop house. You will then need some help on ladders in the middle to help the plastic move along as it goes up and over.

Once the plastic is draped over the frame, pull it into alignment, and then you will need to secure it. You can wrap the extra plastic around 1x2 pieces of wood and then anchor to hip boards or the ground frame.

You will then need to frame in the ends. 2x3 or 2x4 tends to work best. Alternatively, you can drape plastic across the front and back and have it secured, and then have one end fixed so that you can open it when you need to go in and out.

Chapter 7: Multi-Span Greenhouse

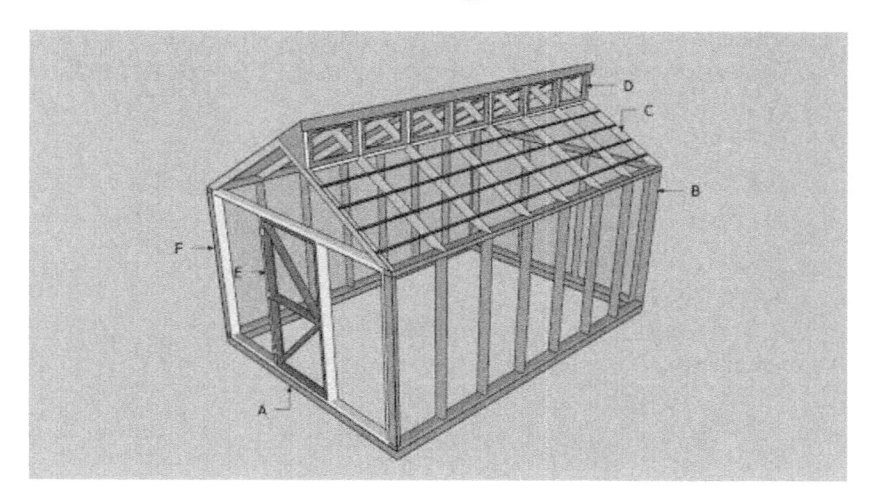

This next greenhouse is eight feet by ten feet and stands 8'6" off of the ground at its highest point. The frame of this greenhouse is made out of mainly 2x4s. A lot of these are built with 2x3s, but 2x4s are easier to find. We'll go over wood stock sizes in a bit. The door is also wider so that a wheelbarrow can fit through if you need to.

It also has two windows that open, which is different than any other greenhouse we will go over in this book. It sits flat on the ground and is held into place with a few stakes located around the bottom that gets hammered into the ground and are nailed into the sides of the greenhouse's base. If you wanted to, you could permanently install it, but there's no real need for that.

It is best to place the greenhouse where it is going to get plenty of sun, especially during the winter. Make sure that you don't place it somewhere where water pools. If it's in a low lying area, you may need to add a drain to help water flow away from the area.

Materials

- 330 ft worth of 2x4 treated wood for the frame. Some of this will get ripped down for parts of the doors and windows.
- 36 ft worth of 4x4 treated wood for the base.
- 10 ft worth of 1x8 treated wood for the fascia.
- A sheet of 4'x8'x3/8" treated plywood for the gussets.
- 350 sq ft ultra-violet-resistant polythene for the covering.
- Latches, handles, hinges, strapping, galvanized plats, and nails

Tools

- Drill
- Level
- Square
- Circular saw
- Jigsaw

Building The Greenhouse

You will start out making the base of your greenhouse. Using the 4x4 wood, create an eight-foot by ten-foot rectangle. Attach the wood together in the corners with nails and nail plates. Make sure the rectangle is square by measuring the diagonals. If they are equal, then it's square.

Before you place the base where it is going to stay, ensure the ground is level and firm. Use some sort of level to figure out the ground's grade and dig out the ground as much as you need to in order to level it off.

You can place the base once the area is flat and driving in stakes around it to secure it to the ground. Nail the stakes into the base and then cut the tops off the stakes to protrude over the base.

Next, you will build the side walls. You will use 2x4s for all of the framing. You will need two 10 foot long boards, five 5 foot long boards, and a brace. On the longboards, make the marks across each at two-foot increments. Then attach the five-foot long boards at the marks and one at each end. Once you have the wall squared in, cut a piece of wood to be the brace so that it fits diagonally across half of the wall. You are going to need to make two of these.

Next, you are going to work on the roof frame sections. You are going to be makeup five roof sections that reach from side-wall to side-wall. You are going to need five long rafters at 73 3/8" long, five short rafters at 53 5/8" long, and five rafter uprights at 11 3/8" long. On the long rafter, cut one end at 60 degrees and the other end at 30 degrees. Do the same on the short rafter, but the 30-degree angle should be angled in the opposite direction to the other angle. On the upright, cut both ends at a 30-degree angle.
You will also need to cut five triangular gussets from your plywood. All three sides should be 20" long.

With that ready, you can make the five roof sections. Take the long rafter and attach the upright rafter at the end with the 30-degree cut so that you have a 1.75" overhang. Take the short rafter at attach the 30-degree end to the long rafter with the upright rafter resting on top. Before securely attaching it, measure to see if the ends of the rafters are eight feet apart. Attach the boards together and then place gusset over the triangle that you made when you put the upright between the long and short rafters. Repeat this on the other four sections.

Next, stand your sidewalls up on the baseboards and use some temporary props to support them. Attach the bottom plate of your sidewalls onto the base of the greenhouse with nails. Do this on both sides. Then raise one of the roof sections and attach it to the top of the side walls at one end. Then place another roof section at the other end of the walls. Us nails to fasten the roof frames to the top plate of the walls. Place the other three roof frames equally spaced across the top of the walls.

Take a ten-foot-long piece of 2x4 and attach it to the upright rafters. This is the window support plate. Then take a ten-foot-long 1x8 and attach it to the top ends of the long rafters. You need to make sure that all of the roof sections are parallel to one another and vertical. You will then need to tuck some galvanized metal window flashing under and behind the fascia before you nail down the 1x8.

On the side of the roof that won't have any windows, brace the rook with two metal straps that run diagonally across the roof. Nail the strap down at the ends and where it crosses over the rafter.

Now you are going to be making the end wall frames. Most of this is just going to be measuring and cutting. You will need a top and bottom plate on either side of what will become a door. You will also need a brace that goes across those sections. You'll also have to make the doorframe. The main thing is to make sure that the door studs are placed 36.75" apart so that the door will feet. The door head, which is the top of the frame, needs to be 72.75" above the base. This is the same process for the front and the back. You will have two doors in the greenhouse.

Next, you will be making your doors. You will need two 2x2 pieces that are six inches long. You can get the 2x2s by ripping down a 2x4 that you haven't used. You will also need three 2x4 pieces cut at three feet long. You will also need to place a plywood gusset wherever you put the door frame pieces together. Attach the three shorter pieces between the longer pieces, making sure the door stays square. Then place the six gussets over the seams. Make two of these. Place three hinges on each door along with a handle or lock to secure the door in place. Hang the doors on the greenhouse.

Next, you will be making your windows. You are going to need two five-foot-long pieces of 2x2 and three 10 inch pieces of 2x4.On the piece that will be the bottom of your window, cut the long end at a 30-degree angle so that it matches the pitch of the roof. Attach the top and bottom window pieces together with the three shorter pieces. You will need to make two of these. Attach the windows to the frame using two butt hinges per window. Place a latch on each of the windows. Cut a section of wood that will act as blocking that will run below the windows between the roof frame.

You will then need to cover your greenhouse with UV-resistant polythene. To keep the covering place, place a really thin piece of wood, known as battens, over the polythene, making sure that the polythene is taut. Nail the battens onto the green studs, the roof rafter, or any other solid piece of wood. You should also cover the windows and doors with this as well.

Most hardware and garden supply stores will only have standard plastic polythene that isn't UV resistant, but if you ask them, they should be able to point you in the right direction as to where you can find the polythene you need for your greenhouse.

Chapter 8: A-Frame Greenhouse

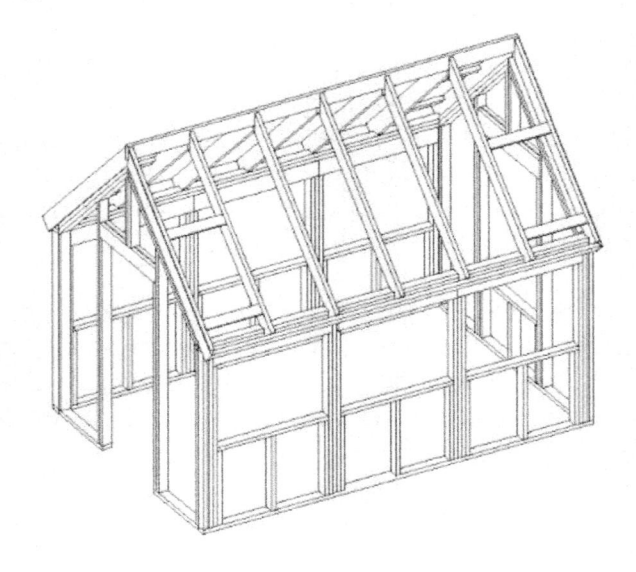

This greenhouse DIY will provide you with a 10x16 size greenhouse, so it's a medium-sized growing area and would be great for a backyard. This is a general rule for all greenhouses, but you need to think about its position. You want to make sure it will get plenty of sunlight during the day. Plants have to have morning sunlight to develop properly. Make sure there aren't a lot of trees or buildings that will end up shading your greenhouse. Also, if needed, level off the ground so that you have a flat surface to build on.

If you would like your greenhouse to last, make sure that you pick out the best materials. Purchase pressure-treated lumber or cedar, and make sure your beams and studs are perfectly straight. If you would like your greenhouse to last, make sure that you pick out the best materials. Purchase pressure-treated lumber or cedar, and make sure your beams and studs are perfectly straight. Also, make sure to exam the wood you get so that you don't get any piece of it with visible signs of damage. It's also important you use proper technique to join the wood properly and make sure you use a level to ensure everything is straight. Theoretically, if you have everything you need, you should be able to get this done in a single weekend.

Materials

- Hinges and latch
- Thermostat outlet
- Vent opener
- Preferred greenhouse covering
- 2.5" screws
- Three 2x2 pieces of lumber – 8'
- 2x6 piece of lumber – 16'
- 46 2x4 pieces of lumber – 8'
- Four 2x4 pieces of lumber – 10'
- Four 2x4 pieces of lumber – 16'
- Two 4x4 pieces of lumber – 10'
- Two 4x4 pieces of lumber – 16'

Tools

- Drill and drill bits
- Chalk line, carpentry pencil, level, and tape measure
- Miter saw or jigsaw
- Glasses and safety gloves

Building the Greenhouse

The first step is to create the base of your greenhouse. You will be using the 4x4 lumber for this. You will have two pieces that are 192" long and two that are 120" long. Again, make sure you have it positioned in a good location because you aren't going to want to move it once it's built. It should get at least eight hours of direct sunlight each day. You should also remove any grass from underneath before you attach the beams. You will use 24" long 2x4 stakes to anchor the base to the ground. The stakes should be placed every 36" apart.

To attach the wood for the base together, you are going to cut a notch into each end of the beams. On one end, draw a line 3.5" in from the end of the beam. Then from the top of the beam, draw a line down 1.75" to connect it to the other line. Do this on every end of all four beams for the base. Then take your circular saw and cut the notches out. Make sure you use parallel cuts to keep this even. Smooth the recess out with some sandpaper. Then connect the beams together and attach them with screws. Make sure that the corners are right-angled.

Next, you will start to make the sidewalls for your greenhouse. The lumber for this should be 2x4. You need two 192" long pieces and nine 72" long pieces. On the long lumber pieces, create seven marks across the lumber, spaced 22.25" apart. Then attach the 72" studs between the long beams at this mark and one at either end. Make sure that your corners are square and everything is flush. You will repeat this for the other sidewall.

Then, you will start building the front and back walls for the greenhouse. Working with 2x4 pieces of lumber, you will need two 113" long pieces and five 72" long pieces. Do the same as last time, and make three marks along both long boards spaces 22.25" apart. Then attach the studs between the beams at those marks and one at either end.

Next, you will start to raise the walls. You will need four pieces of 2x4's to use as a temporary brace. With a level, make sure that one of the walls is up and square with the base. Use the temporary brace, one at each end, to hold the wall into place. Do the same on the other side.

You will then raise the front and back walls. Raise the front, using a level to make sure everything is straight, and attach the adjacent studs together using screws. Do the same for the back wall. You can take the temporary braces off now.

You will now start to build the roof of your greenhouse. You will build the top ridge first. You will need two 28.75" 2x4 pieces and one 192" long 2x6. Find the center of the front wall and attach one of the 2x4 pieces to the top of the front wall. Do the same thing on the back wall with the other 2x4. Then take the long piece of lumber and attach it to the tops of the pieces you just put up. Make sure that the thin side of the 2x6 is the one facing up. Once again, make sure everything is lined up correctly and level.

Next, you will start getting the rafters ready for the roof. You will use 2x4 pieces of lumber. The rafters will need to be 68.5" long. You will cut one end at a 60-degree angle and the other end at a 30-degree angle. You will need to make 18 of these.

Then you need to attach the rafters. Each rafter will connect to the top of the wall at a stud and then connect to the top ridge's side. Make sure that the edges are flush and the rafters stay spaced equally apart.

Then, you are going to build your door. You will be using 2x2 pieces of lumber. You need two 69" long pieces, 2 26.5" long pieces, one 23.5" piece, and two 41" long pieces. Frame in the door by attaching the 69" pieces and 26.5" pieces. Measure and find the center point of the door and attach the 23.5" board in the middle. Take the 41" pieces and cut one end of each at 55.5 and cut the other end of each at 34.5. Then place these diagonally in the door squares. Attach with screws.

The door will then be attached between two studs on the front of your greenhouse. Use three hinges to secure the door to the frame of the greenhouse. You should also install a lock on the door to keep in place and prevent it from swinging open.
Check your frame for any rough edges. You can go through and fill drill holes with wood putty. You should also go over all corners and edges with some sandpaper to smooth out any rough edges. You can also apply a couple of exterior paint or stain coats to the wood to help prevent decaying and water damage.

Lastly, you should use translucent polyethylene foil or sheets. Spread this across the frame, keeping it as tight as possible, and use a staple gun to attach it to the wood. Make sure you place the staples six inches apart to make sure you don't have any significant gaps. You also have other options for covering your greenhouse, but using a polyethylene sheet is the easiest and usually the most inexpensive. They also last longer. You can use glass, depending on where you live, but that often gets expensive.

Chapter 9: Post and Rafter

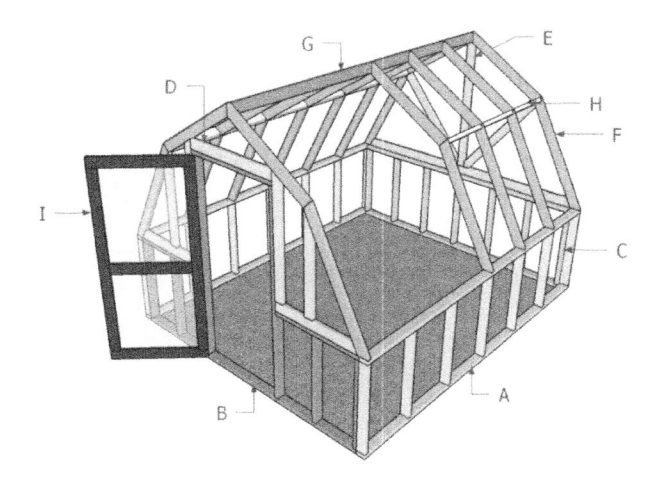

The last greenhouse we are going to go over how to build is the post and rafter greenhouse. This is a common greenhouse structure and is one of the strongest since rafters support the roof. However, this is probably one of the most labor-intensive projects. If you are looking to save money when building your greenhouse, the best thing to do is repurpose old lumber and check with businesses who work on windows or something like that to see if they have inventory that they can't sell that they are willing to sell to you at a reduced price. This particular post and rafter is shaped like a barn.

When it comes to picking our lumber, even if you are reusing old wood, make sure that the planks are still right. They should be straight and have no visible decay, twists, knots, or cracks. Always make sure you are using a level and align the components correctly before drilling in the screws; otherwise, it won't be symmetrical. Once you have all of the materials needed, you can theoretically finish this project in about a day.

Materials

- Hinges and latch
- Thermostat outlet
- Vent opener
- Preferred greenhouse covering
- 500 pieces of 2.5" screws
- 41 2x4 pieces of lumber – 8 ft
- Five 2x4 pieces of lumber – 12 ft
- Four 2x4 pieces of lumber – 10 ft

This is how to breakdown the materials for the blueprint.
- A – 2 2x4 pieces of lumber – 144" long, seven pieces – 33" long X2 sides
- B – 2x4 piece of lumber – 113" long, four pieces – 33" long, two pieces – 36.5" long, two pieces 76.25" long, one piece – 40" long (front)
- C – 2 2x4 pieces of lumber – 113" long, seven pieces – 33" long (back)
- D – 2x4 piece of lumber – 36" long, two pieces – 35.5" long, two pieces – 43.25" long, one piece – 40" long (front)
- E – 2x4 piece of lumber – 112" long, two pieces – 47.5" long, one piece – 54.75" long (back)
- F – 14 2x4 pieces of lumber – 41.5" long, 14 pieces – 48" long (rafters)
- G – 2x4 – 1414: long (top ridge)
- H – 12 2x4 pieces of lumber – 22.25" long (blockings)
- I – 2 2x4 pieces of lumber – 37" long, two pieces – 69.25" long, one piece – 30" long (door)

Tools

- Safety glasses
- Safety gloves
- Sander
- Screwdriver
- Drill machinery
- Miter saw
- Level
- Framing square
- Tape measure
- Hammer

Building The Greenhouse

The first thing you are going to do is build the side walls. Cut the parts that you need out of your 2x4 lumber. You will need two 2x4's at 144" long and seven 2x4's at 33" long. On the two longer pieces of lumber, mark 22.25" spaces across the boards. This is where the shorter pieces will go. Drill two pilot holes, one at each edge, into each of the marks, including at both ends of the boards. Now fit the shorter pieces, or studs, on the boards and drill screws through the pilot holes into the studs. Make sure that you have the corners square before inserting your screws. You will repeat this for the second sidewall.

Next, you will build the rafters. You will need a miter saw for this to cut the angles. Take a 41.5" long piece of 2x4 and a 48" piece of 2x4. At one end of each, use the miter saw to cut the end to a 60-degree angle. At the other end of each, cut at a 75-degree angle. Attach the two pieces of wood together at the ends with the 75-degree cuts. You will need to drill pocket holes to attach them together. Alternatively, you can use .75" plywood gussets to reinforce the joints. Make four of these.

After that, you will attach one rafter to each end of the side walls. The longer end of the rafter will attach to the top of the sidewall. Make sure the corners are square and attach with screws. Once you have a rafter attached to each end of the one side wall, repeat on the other sidewall. You will then take a 141" 2x4 to attach the two sides of the greenhouse together. This is your top ridge.

Then, you'll make ten more rafters. You will use the same process as before, except your wood pieces need to be 40.75" long and 48" long. Keep the 75, and 60 degree cuts the same.
Next, you can fit the rafters into the structure. Each rafter should be spaced 22.25" apart, just like the studs were done in the side walls.

You will then add the blocking into the roof of the greenhouse. These are 22.25" pieces of 2x4's that will be placed between each rafter where the two pieces of wood were attached. Drill pocket holes at either end and secure them with 2.5" screws. Make sure that you keep the edges flushes before you insert your screw.

With the main structure of the greenhouse built, we'll create the front wall. You will need a 113" long 2x4 that will serve as the bottom of the wall. You should also have four 33" long pieces, 2 36.5" long pieces, 2 76.25" pieces, and one 40" long piece.

On your longest board, measure 16.75" in from the edge and place a mark. From that mark, measure another 16.75" and make another mark. Make this same measurement one more time. Then move to the other edge of the board and make the same two marks at 16.75". These are where your studs are going to go, as well as the doorframe.

At either end of the longest board, attach a 33" 2x4. Attach your remaining 2 33" boards at the first marks you made on the long board. At the last two marks you made, attach the 76.25" 2x4's. Make sure that all of the edges are flush and square.

Attach the 36.5" boards on top of the studs. Make sure you attach the edges to the doorframe as well. Then finish out the doorframe by attaching the 40" 2x4 to the top.

Next, attach the front wall to the body of the greenhouse. Make sure that the wall is level and that the corners are square, and connect with screws in the studs. The top of the doorframe won't be attached just yet.

You'll need a miter saw again. Take two 36" 2x4's and cut one end of each at a 60-degree angle. Attach this to the top of the front wall, above the studs. The two-inch edge should be placed along the edge of the front wall with the angled edge snuggly placed against the rafters.

Take two 35.5" 2x4's and cut one end of each at a 60-degree angle. The angled end will rest against the rafters, where the two pieces of wood were attached. Then secure the other end into the 2x4 you placed in the last step. This should be done on both sides of the door.

Next, take a 40" 2x4 and attach it to the top of the doorframe. The top corners of the board should touch the rafters. The next step will secure the doorframe.

Next, take two 43.25" 2x4's and cut one end of each at a 30-degree angle. Secure these two pieces of wood on either side of the doorframe. The doorframe should now be securely attached to the rafters. Make sure there are no gaps and that everything is square.

Then you will build the back wall. You will need 2 113" 2x4's and 7 33" 2x4's. Like you did on the sides, attach the studs 17" apart, making sure they were square and flush. To finish off the back of the greenhouse, you will need 2 45.5" 2x4's and a 54.75" 2x4.

You'll need to do some mitering here as well. At one end of one of the shorter pieces, you will create a point by making 2 15 degree cuts on either side of the one end. Do the same on one end of the other shorter piece. At the other end of these shorter pieces, you will need to make a 90-degree angle. Then, at one end of the 54.75" 2x4, create a point by cutting a 60-degree angle on either side of the edge.

Set those aside for now. Take a 112" 2x4 and cut each end at a 60-degree angle. Placing the two-inch end on top of the back wall, attach this piece to the back wall making sure the angled ends fit snuggly against the rafters.

Next, take the 54.75" 2x4 you prepared earlier, place the flat end against the piece you just attached, and then screw the pointed end into the rafters. The other two pieces will be placed at an angle on either side of this piece.

The 90-degree end will fit between the vertical and horizontal pieces of wood, and the 15-degree point will fit into the corner of the rafter.

Next, you'll build the door. You'll need 2 69.25" 2x4's, 2 37" 2x4's, and one 30" 2x4. Attach the 37" pieces to the top and bottom of the 69.25" pieces. Decide on which end is the top of your door and measure down 34.75" of an inch. Place the 30" piece between the longer pieces at this point. You can then fit the door to the doorframe using two hinges. Then attach your door latch to lock your door.

You can finish this out by covering the holes with some woody putty and smoother out the surface with 120-grit sandpaper. You can also paint or stain the wood if you would like.

To finish building your greenhouse, you will need to cover it. This part is up to you. You can choose to use windows to fill in the spaces or cover with a film. The easiest method would be to use greenhouse plastic. This won't tear easily, and it withstands all weather conditions. All you need to do to attach the plastic is to use 3/8-inch staples to fasten it to the frame every six inches. Make sure you stretch the plastic as tight as you can get it.

Chapter 10: Keeping Your Greenhouse Running

Having a greenhouse can be the most satisfying thing that you have ever done. You can have one just about anywhere, in a city, a suburb, or on a farm. There are some pride and gratitude that come from watching seeds and cuttings grow into plants, and before you realize what happened, you have plants that will feed you and your family.

What Plants to Grow

The first thing you have to decide is what plants you want to grow and how many you want. If you are brand new to greenhouse gardening, you should probably begin with just one crop. If you begin growing an assortment of plants, it might be more than you can handle since each plant will have its own shade, fertilizing, spraying and watering requirement. You don't need all that hassle when you could just grow 10,000 of a specific plant just as easily as 3,000 plants of various types.

When you are trying to figure out what plants you want to grow, you need to know your ability to grow plants first. Then you have to figure out how many plants you are able to grow and how much it will cost you to grow the plants. Knowing how much it will cost to produce your plants will help you figure out which plants to grow.

Sowing Seeds

When you have figured out which plants you want to grow, you need to sow the seeds either in pots, boxes, or outside. If you are a new grower, begin putting them in pots. These are best for seeds that germinate slowly. It will be easy to see and get rid of weeds without bothering the seeds. The speed they will germinate depends on the amount of oxygen, moisture, and temperature they get. A seedbed in a shaded area will give them the best temperature because the hot sun could injure or kill the seedlings as they begin to grow. Make sure your soil is well-drained but stays moist to keep the oxygen levels stable. Having good air circulation around the seedlings will keep them from damping off.

The depth at which you sow the seeds will depend on how big they are. The best "rule of thumb" is to plant them at a depth that is three or four times larger than their diameter. If you have very tiny seeds, just sprinkle some on top of the dirt and cover them over lightly with more dirt. When they get large enough, you can transplant them into larger pots. This can "harden" the plant. This allows the plant to handle harsh weather conditions. Sow the seeds in either sand, peat moss, vermiculite, or a combination of these.

Your Greenhouse

The main purpose of having a greenhouse is to get your plants growing faster by keeping the temperature and humidity stable. You can also create the right temperature and light intensity for your crop. This is another good reason to think about growing huge quantities of just a few kinds of plants instead of trying to grow huge amounts of various plants. You shouldn't be scared of experimenting. During the first year of growing plants in a greenhouse, begin some plants in the late winter to have them ready by late spring or early summer. Test some different kinds during the first winter, where temperatures are below zero. This will help you learn more about your greenhouse and how much heat you will need to keep your plants alive.

As for your greenhouse, one that has been designed well and is covered with a double layer of poly will use about 50 percent less heat than a single layer, fiberglass house that most people use. A double poly greenhouse will last you for about four years; a single layer will last around six months. Newer greenhouses with inflated double poly plastic sheets won't cost as much as the polycarbonate, acrylic, and glass greenhouses.

Light Transmission

If you want to make sure your plants get the right amount of sun takes a lot of planning. This will include finding a way to get the best light during winter's cloudy and dark days. You need to stay away from too much light as this can kill your plants if you don't ventilate them properly.

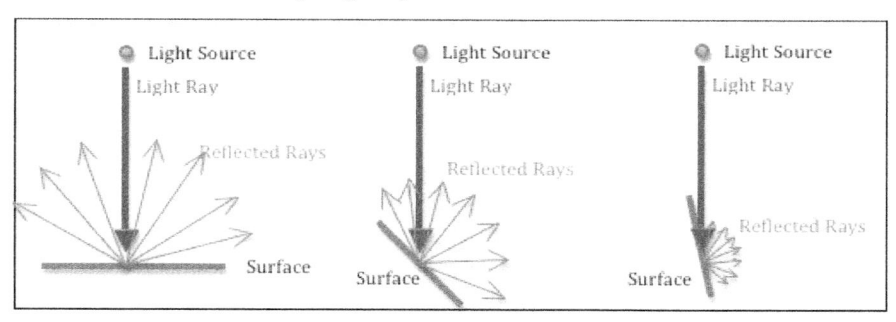

This highest amount of sunlight, which ranges between 90 and 93 percent, can be provided by glass sheets. When the glass has been framed properly, the greenhouse won't be able to transmit more than 70 percent light. When you take into consideration the heating pipes, wiring, and other obstacles, this will lower your light transmission -down to 60 and 70 percent. You do have the choice of using double-poly sheeting or panels made from polycarbonate or acrylic. With some well-designed framing, you could get the same level of light that glass sheets can give you.

In order to figure out the amount of shade your plants are going to need, you could buy a light meter that can help you adjust it to the right degrees. These devices have a numbered guide that is easy to read. Just keep it away from direct sunlight. Keep it in the darker places of your greenhouse and then read the meter. Your readings might change depending on where the sun is located and any reflections.

Shades that you can place over the greenhouse or inside it that you can roll up and down when needed can help you regulate the amount of light your plants get. This cloth will cost you around ten cents per square foot and will last for ten years. When figuring out the amount of light you need to block out, the best choice would be about 65 to 73 percent for any type of foliage plant. Most growers will use 73 percent during the hot summer months and 55 percent during winter.

If you don't use the right amount of shade cloth, your plants could become too dry or sunburned. If you use too much shade, your plants will stay too wet, and this can lead to fungus or other diseases. The amount of shade depends on the plants that you are growing.

Most vegetable and flowering plants will do better during summer under some shade cloth, but you might not need shade during some of the other months. Some landscaping plants will grow great under some light shade. If you grow hanging plants, make sure you hang them between two and three feet apart. You could use between 55 to 75 percent shade. Most people don't realize that plants grown in the shade don't require any shade during the winter.

Shading paint is one more option. These compounds are painted on the outside of your poly-greenhouse cover. You can find several good ones at your local home improvement stores. If you can grow your plants under shade during the last part of their maturity, your plants will be of better quality. You can make a shade house from four by fours and two by fours.

You could use scrap lumber to create one. A cheap one can be made from some 12-foot pressure-treated poles, mobile home anchors, aircraft cables with clamps, and the right size cloth to cover the sides and top. You will set the 12-foot poles about 20 feet apart on each corner, or where you need the most strength. Then stretch the aircraft cable over the top and fasten it to the ground with the mobile home anchors. The entire structure gets covered with cloth, and then the sides and corners are stitched together.

Controlling the Environment

You just can't overestimate how important it is to control your greenhouse's environment. Moving, fresh air is just as crucial to the plants as water and light. It doesn't matter if you are growing your plants hydroponically or in pots; you have to watch the temperature. Temperatures need to stay around 70 to 75 degrees, and the humidity needs to be at 50 percent. If you can keep these levels consistent, your plants will grow faster, have better color, and be of a higher quality.

If you can properly manage the climate inside the greenhouse, the production will normally be more than you ever imagined.

CO_2

Everybody who has ever grown anything knows that carbon dioxide is needed for healthy plants. During the Autumn and Winter months, when you keep your greenhouse closed to keep it warmer, there won't be that much air circulation from outside. You can help your plants grow better by raising the CO_2 levels. Normal concentrations are usually between 250 and 350 ppm. If you can raise the level to between 1200 and 1500 ppm could help your plants grow better. Enriching your plants with carbon dioxide won't replace your good growing skills.

Watering Your Plants

You need to feed your plants the right amount of water. If your plants get too dry, they will quit growing, and this could lead to stunting. You can stay away from this by testing your water for contaminants. This can be done by putting some water in a jar and taking it to your local county extension office to be tested. The first thing in the morning would be the best time. The best way to check for your pots' moisture level is to push your finger into the soil a few inches to see how moist the soil feels. Water the plants so that the soil becomes drenched in the pot. Add a water-soluble fertilizer to your plants once every ten days. Adding some peat moss to the soil will create a soil that holds water better and more constant.

Propagation

If you are growing your plants from seeds, make sure to transplant them when they become seedlings into rock wool, the ground, or a container. This propagation stage will have different requirements and demands for moisture and temperature. If you are growing cuttings, give them an environment that encourages rooting. The best method would be to take cuttings from your existing plants or to buy some. The best plants that grow the best from cuttings are herbs, flowers, foliage plants, shrubs, any type of vine, tomatoes, and cucumbers. Using a rooting hormone on the cuttings can help them take root faster.

Misting

Rooting your cuttings under a mist or spray is a technique that many greenhouse growers and beginners like using. The purpose of this is to keep a film of water on the plant's leaves; this will keep the cuttings strong until they grow enough roots. Once they have established roots, you can expose them to more air and light without hurting them.

Misting can speed up the rooting process, helps plants that are harder to root, and keep diseases away in cuttings by keeping all the fungus spores off the plant before they can attack the plant. Even though the leaves during this process have to be kept moist constantly, you need to keep the amount at a minimum. Too much water could leach out nutrients from the compost and could cause the plant to starve. Overwatering could harm the cutting, so make sure you use nozzles that can produce an extremely fine mist.

You can control the spray in two ways. You could use a time clock mechanism to set a timer to give the plants a burst of spray every five minutes or so. The main problem with this is that the interval between mists has to stay the same despite all the changing weather conditions. If you set the clock to give the plants a burst every five minutes, the plant could become flooded during the dark conditions and become undernourished when it is sunny and bright.

The next method that controls the spray involves an element called "an electronic leaf." This can be used with a switching controller and a solenoid valve that has been installed in the water lines. This artificial leaf gets placed with the cuttings. It will dry out or loses its superficial water at the same rate as the cuttings. At specific stages of dryness, the element will open the solenoid, so water goes to the nozzles. This electronic leaf will cause the valve to close once the spray has moistened it.

Chapter 11: Tips and Tricks

Most beginner greenhouse gardeners are very enthusiastic but don't let this overshadow all the steps you need to take to make sure your efforts are a success. Growing produce in a greenhouse is fulfilling and enjoyable, but it does take some knowledge and skills, and this learning curve could be a bit steep.

As with any new experience, paying attention to all the tiny details while creating a strong foundation is very important. Even if you are growing a hardy variety of plants, there are many variables that can change the growth rate and your chances of having a successful harvest.

It is going to take some patience, but this won't just set you up for success but will help you make an environment that will feed your enthusiasm and help it to bloom. If you are new to greenhouse gardening, it might be hard to do everything right, and even though trial and error are needed to help you learn, these tips can give you a head start.

Starting Seeds Seasonally

The best advantage of having a greenhouse is you get to extend your growing season, give you an early start in summer or spring, and allows you to grow specific vegetables all year long. You must have all the important supplies that you will need to have a successful harvest. You need to buy:

- Water
- Fertilizer
- Sterile soil
- Containers

You will also need a heat source to help grow your seeds at the start of the season when the temperatures are cool. A heating mat is a reasonably cheap and easy way to heat your seed flats to help your plants grow. There are other ways like heat cables that you bury in the seedbeds.

Thermometers

This is another vital piece of equipment that you will need. A thermometer tells you when you need to ventilate your greenhouse, where you need to place some shade or when you need to add some heat, and which areas are the coolest. If you are new to greenhouse gardening, you absolutely need a thermometer.

Lights

During the late part of spring and summer, your greenhouse should be getting all the night it needs for the plants, but if you would like to continue growing during late fall and winter, you are going to need other sources of light if you want your plants to be strong and healthy.

Having LED and high output fluorescent light strips are the most popular since they give out the full light spectrum. They are energy efficient and are able to cover a large area.

If you are on a tight budget or are growing small crops, a normal fluorescent light strip that is hanging between three and seven inches above your plants will be just fine.

Keep Your Greenhouse Tidy

This might seem like nothing more than another chore, but when you put things in their proper place, you will be able to find what you need at a glance. You will be able to walk into your greenhouse and see your pots, soil, fertilizer, etc. You will always have enough space to put your plants once you placed them in a pot. Having piles of equipment lying all over the place invites slugs, snails, and other pests into your space.

Heating

You will need to heat your greenhouse during the colder months, and this could be a bit of a learning experience. For anyone who is new to greenhouse gardening, it would be best to use electric heaters since they are easy to install, they are cheaper, and can be used in various ways. A small heater can heat a smaller greenhouse without any problems. Larger greenhouses are going to need a 240 plus volt heater that can be controlled by a waterproof, reliable thermostat.

Gas heaters can work, too, but they aren't as economical, and you have to make sure you have the right ventilation and a constant supply of fresh air so it will burn. You also have to make sure your exhaust the fumes.

For people who like being nice to the environment, some ways don't use as much energy, but you will have to set up ventilation systems that use any unneeded warmth from your house. Some growers will use large rocks to absorb the sun's heat during the day and release it during the night. Even if you use supplementary sources of heat, these methods are great ways of keeping the temperature inside your greenhouse constant during the day.

How Much Space Do Your Plants Need

You have to be ready for your plants by figuring out how much room your plants are going to need. If you crowd them, it could cause them to compete for light and space. This stress could introduce your plants to insects and diseases.

Cooling

When the heat is unbearable during the middle of summer, it could be a bit hard to keep your greenhouse at a constant temperature. Since they have been designed to keep heat in, cooling them down is a lot harder.

This means you have to regularly and continuously measure the temperature inside your greenhouse during the hot months is very important. Regularly measuring the temperature of your greenhouse could mean the difference between regulating the temperature just by opening the door or using some type of cooling device. If your greenhouse overheats regularly, you can use evaporative air coolers that help keep humidity levels consistent.

Begin With Seeds Instead of Cuttings or Seedlings

The best way to reduce getting diseases, mites, or other insects is, to begin with, seeds that you plant inside your greenhouse. If you get cuttings or seedlings from another place, you could be bringing in things that can hurt your plants. You should seed more plants than how many you want since all the seeds aren't going to germinate, and this could help give you a healthy plant selection to start.

Ventilation

Seasonality plays a large role in ventilating a greenhouse of any size. During summer months, convection currents that are created by all the natural heat from the sun will keep good circulation. If you keep the roof and wall vents open during the summer, cool air gets pulled in through the wall vents while the hot air escapes out the roof vents, and this draws a constant fresh air supply.

During the winter, keeping air constantly circulating to prevent mold from growing can be hard to do. Be sure you don't overwater the plants. Most growers will keep a fan running during the cold months. Oscillating fans work best for this.

Grow Things That Need to Be Grown Inside a Greenhouse

Try to grow something that can only thrive in a greenhouse, like heat-loving vegetables or tropical flowers. This will add some interest to your greenhouse but having the success of growing unique plants can be very exhilarating.

Begin With Plants That Are Easy to Grow
Starting your greenhouse efforts with plants that are easy to grow can help give your confidence a boost. Coleus, basil, and lettuce are some good options. You can move on to hot peppers, eggplant, cucumbers, and tomatoes once you have some experience under your belt. If you are a beginner, stay away from trees and bushes since they take up more space and take a lot longer to grow.

Watering
The biggest mistake that beginners make is watering their plants according to a schedule. There are several variables that dictate when your plants need to be watered. The growth stage, humidity, and temperature all affect the amount of water you need.
If it is in the middle of winter, you probably only need to water them every ten days or so. During the summer months, you will need to increase the frequency. The easiest way for you to know when to water your plants is to measure the soil's moisture. You can use a moisture meter or by feeling the soil.

Keep Pests Away
Besides not buying plants from other places, you can install insect screens on your air intakes to keep pests outside. You could keep your outside plants away from the greenhouse. Do anything you have to do to your outdoor garden once you have taken care of all your inside plants. Keep your pets away from the greenhouse, too, as they could bring in diseases or insects.

Chapter 12: Myths About Greenhouse Gardening

Now that we have covered some tips to help you get your greenhouse up and going, here are some myths about greenhouse gardening. Have you ever had a friend that still believes in sirens? Did your grandmother think that aloe vera heals absolutely everything?

Myths can be impressive, and they are usually based on some facts that might or might not have been real at some point. Still, people have believed in them for so long that they get stronger over time and get passed down from generation to generation until it turns into a tradition. This is an ancestral and unbreakable law.

The truth of the matter is in the world we live in, where technology and science are responsible for making us more cultured, we do believe in some things that aren't totally true.

For many years all the myths about greenhouse gardening have ruined its reputation. From not having any taste to misusing resources, growing crops inside a greenhouse have been crucified as the biggest sin to greenhouse gardening.

It is time that we break through all those myths.

- **Pesticides Are Used**

For many years, industrialization and technological advances have been synonymous with pollution and damaging the environment. But our generation has seen the effects of mistreating the planet.

There are some strict regulations about the products that you might or might not use. One of them is pesticides. This is because their job is to kill. Even if they could, they aren't as selective as we would like them to be. Most of them will just attack the pests that they were designed to kill, but they can negatively affect the ecosystem.

It was thought that greenhouse gardening used many pesticides, but we can honestly say that this isn't true. There have been many developments in keeping greenhouse gardening practices safe not only for us but also for the environment. Nobody within the greenhouse community uses pesticides in their greenhouses.

- **Greenhouse Plants Don't Taste Good**

Who wants to eat a tomato that doesn't taste delicious? What about an onion without any flavor? For several years, there was a myth circulating that produce grown in a greenhouse didn't have any flavor.

I'm here to tell you that this is completely false. It is actually the total opposite. All the advances in growing crops inside a greenhouse have been giving us tremendous results recently.

Foods grown inside a greenhouse give you tastier and healthier crops than the ones grown the traditional way.

- **Growing Inside Greenhouses Isn't Natural**

When you hear this kind of statement, you can understand why this isn't anything more than another myth. It seems like anytime somebody mentions a greenhouse, everybody thinks about an evil scientist doing weird experiments to make their plants grow big and tall.

There isn't anything in the world that is farther from the truth. If your greenhouse has lots of direct sunlight, your plants are going to receive all the heat they are going to need, so you shouldn't need any type of artificial lighting or heating.

You really have to quit believing in myths about greenhouses because everything that gets grown inside a greenhouse is 100 percent natural.

- **Water Gets Wasted**

This is one of the most common myths about greenhouses, but it is also totally false. You don't need to think about it too much since there are enough facts to prove it. There isn't a cultivation system where water gets appreciated how greenhouses appreciate it. Farmers who work in greenhouses are very meticulous managers over this precious resource.

For every crop grown in a greenhouse, the top layer of soil is usually sand, which lets the plant break the capillarity. This is a liquid property that makes them either fall or rise through a capillary tube because of their intermolecular strength. The best way to understand this is by thinking of it as plants sucking the water out of the soil through their roots.

This keeps the water from leaking or being evaporated unintentionally. If this isn't enough to prove it to you, here are some technological advances to support this. Most greenhouses today have been equipped with computer-controlled irrigation systems. This allows you to take advantage of every drop of water.

Thanks to all of these advances, greenhouse crops will consume about half the amount of water that normal crops that are grown outside.

- **Greenhouse Gardening Can't Be Modernized**

After what I have covered above, this myth is even more absurd. Even though this technology might seem to be reserved for other areas, most experts are still developing better solutions to optimize this method.

All these developments are done inside greenhouses. Some examples are water-based, wind, and solar electricity systems. Why do we need all these things? The main reason is the practical problems. There is an urgent need for us to make the most out of all the natural resources that we have available to us.

Because of this, we can go even farther than we ever thought possible with greenhouse gardening. Using pesticides can be eliminated, along with being able to improve our crops and using rainwater better.

Chapter 13: Mistakes Made By Beginner Gardeners

You know by now that it is possible to extend your growing season by growing food inside a greenhouse. Growing crops inside a greenhouse lets you enjoy fresh herbs and produce all year long. Having a reliable greenhouse that will last you several years is a great investment. Most beginning gardeners will make some common mistakes that can turn their investment into a storage space. Don't allow this to happen to you.

With some planning and knowledge, you can set yourself up for success while you enjoy a greenhouse full of plants and food.

1. Picking the Wrong Greenhouse

All greenhouses are not created equal. Several factors can help you figure out which one would be best for you. With all the confusing options out there, it might be hard for you to know all the things that matter and the things that don't.

The greenhouses that don't cost too much, like hoop houses, are easy for you to put together by yourself. You can grow a variety of food in them, and they are fairly inexpensive. This is a very tempting place for new greenhouse gardeners. While you might not be spending as much time or money upfront, they won't last as long as other types. They can be damaged by high winds or heavy snow. They might not extend your growing season like you thought they would. They do cost a lot to keep hot and cold, and you will have to replace the cover often. Even though your upfront costs are low, maintaining, operating, and repairing your greenhouse will be a lot higher. If you aren't sure if greenhouse gardening is right for you, it might make more sense to experiment with some of these greenhouses before you jump right in.

If you know without a shadow of a doubt that you want to have a garden all year long, a higher-quality, more expensive greenhouse is what you should choose. Even though some of these cost more at the beginning, they will be stronger and last a long time. If you want to grow your own food, your ROI could be offset in a couple of years by saving you money on fresh produce.

Answer the following questions to help you decide which greenhouse would be best for you:

- Would you like to experiment with not much money down to see if you like greenhouse gardening?
- Do you want to stay away from future expenses and hassles by building a greenhouse that will last you a long time so you can begin planting?
- Will you be using your greenhouse for other activities like reading, meditation, or yoga?
- What is the climate where you live?
- Would you like to extend your growing season for a couple of months, or would you like to grow your food all year long?
- Do you how a budget, and how much can you spend on cooling and heating?
- How many people will you be feeding?
- How much outdoor space do you have for your greenhouse?

The way you answer the above questions will help you figure out the kind of greenhouse that suits your situation. Think about your gardening goals, and be sure you get a greenhouse that will match your lifestyle and needs.

2. Picking the Wrong Place

After you have figured out the right greenhouse for you, where will you put it? Do you have room on a north slope of a hill in your backyard? You might be shocked by how many new gardeners pick the worst spot possible.

Because many gardeners begin gardening lives outside, they take pride in their outdoor spots. They mark the ground, get the soil ready, and place a fence around it to keep critters out. There is a lot of analysis that goes into finding the right spot with the right amount of sunlight since sunlight is needed for any garden.

Most of these accomplished forget to factor in the sun when they change their gardening into a greenhouse. Just like growing anything outside, you need to have the right amount of sun hitting your plants inside the greenhouse. Pay attention to the sun's angle on the location you chose. Be sure they are getting the right exposure to the sun. Think about all the objects that might block the sun like neighbors' houses, buildings, or trees. You need to know the sun's path throughout the day and the seasons for your location.

You also need to think about the greenhouse's design since greenhouses will get hot. If you aren't careful, the greenhouse might get too hot and kill your plants. You could solve this problem by putting your greenhouse in the shade of a tree.

During the summer, the tree's leaves will block out some of the sun, and in winter, the tree will drop its leaves to let more sunlight to reach the plants. This can be a bit risky because it is hard to know just how much heat and light a tree can block during the summer. Once you find that sweet spot, it can help you regulate the temperature. There are some other ways that we will discuss a bit later.

3. Planting In Bad Soil

Think about buying a greenhouse, building it, and putting all kinds of plants into it, and all of a sudden, you have aphids, whiteflies, and crickets. After all your hard work, research, and planning, having a greenhouse that doesn't produce anything can be heartbreaking. Beginner gardeners make this mistake. When you don't make sure you have healthy soil before you plant your seeds, it will waste your time, money, and effort.

When all is said and done, your greenhouse needs to give you the best place to grow your plants so you can give them what they need, and that is decent soil. I'm not talking about the dirt you have your normal plants in. I'm talking bout mineral-rich soil that has living nutrients in it. There is a direct relationship between your soil's health, your plants' health, and your body's health.

To stay away from getting frustrated and wasting your money on resources, you need to invest in the best soil you can from the start. Put it into your budget. It doesn't make any sense to put money into a greenhouse just to fill it with dead dirt. Buy the best soil you can find. It will be the best investment in your gardening happiness and your health.

4. Planting Too Many Things

Once you have the perfect greenhouse built on that perfect spot in your backyard, you have filled it with fertile soil; you now want to fill it up with plants. That was the main reason behind this, right? You want to fill every speck of soil with transplants and seeds. You want to turn around and see some kind of plant everywhere you look. You want to grow a bumper crop from the get-go. But wise gardeners will inform you that you need to "resist the temptation."

Yes, greenhouses give you many advantages, but it isn't without some challenges. When you move your plants inside, you are losing some beneficial qualities to growing your plants outside that you probably don't realize. Inside greenhouses, you don't have a gentle breeze. You have to create some air circulation by opening windows, doors, or by turning on fans. With all the limited air circulation, plant density becomes crucial.

Having the correct spaces between plants is very important, whether you are growing outside or inside. Inside a greenhouse, it is important to pay attention to how densely your plants are growing. Leaving your plants close together could spell disaster. You have to make sure you keep lots of air circulating around your plants.

5. Watering Too Often or Too Much

Watering your greenhouse plants might turn out to be your new meditation practice. There is just something that is deeply fulfilling about tending to a garden. Watering can get you moving; it activates your senses and makes you observe your surroundings. You get to smell the richness of the soil, see the green of the plants, and smell all the fragrant blossoms. Watering your plants can lull you into a peaceful place.

But you might kill your plants if you aren't careful. The soil's water retention, temperature, and humidity are unique to every greenhouse. It is easy to saturate your soil and inadvertently drown your plants. Watering too much can lead to mold, weak plants, and invites in diseases, bugs, and pests.

To make sure that you don't water too much, use a moisture meter to keep track. These are fairly cheap and work great. They can save your plants while decreasing your water bill and helps you keep your peace of mind.

Check the soil in your plants with a moisture meter before you water. Remember that different plants will have different needs, so you have to check every single plant. With some research and diligence, you could keep your soil at the optimum moisture level to make your plants healthy and strong.

6. Temperature Control

Some of the more expensive greenhouses have many built-in features like temperature control. Some come equipped with windows that will automatically open, vents that automatically open, solar-powered air circulation, and a built-in solar heat sink that can regulate the temperature inside.

If the greenhouse you picked didn't come with all the above benefits, shade cloth is a great way to cut down on your heating and lighting bill during the summer. You can find some that are fairly inexpensive, and depending on the greenhouse, they are easy to install during the summer and remove during the cooler months. A shade cloth that is placed right can reduce light penetration by 50 percent without depriving light plants.

Another good way to keep your greenhouse cooler during the summer is to harness your plant's power of transpiration.

During the summer, the garden beds will get hot. If there is any soil exposed, it will heat up and acts like a thermal heat sink. This, in turn, radiates heat throughout the greenhouse. You will need to keep your beds shaded during the summer.

The best way to do this is by planting some plants with large foliage that gives the interior some shade during the summer. My favorite is to plant a fig tree. They grow great inside a greenhouse, and they have large leaves that can shade the garden beds during the hotter months. They are deciduous and will shed their leaves during the winter when you want the most heat and light that you can get. If you are using your greenhouse all year long, fig trees are a great addition to your greenhouse or garden.
When you can keep your greenhouse cool during the summer by using plants with large foliage, you will get the best of transpiration. Plants can move a lot of water. They can pull moisture from the soil and pump it through their flowers, leaves, and stems. So that fig tree isn't just deciduously delicious, but it can shade the soil and keeps your greenhouse cooler.

Greenhouse gardening is a great experience. You are able to extend your growing season, and according to the kind of greenhouse you pick, you could even grow food all year long. It is very fulfilling to have a warm haven where you can grow whatever you want, no matter what the weather is outside. If you can stay away from the mistakes above, you can enjoy a peaceful oasis and fresh food all year long.

PART III

PRODUCING PRODUCE YEAR-ROUND

You're just one step away from being a Greenhouse Gardening Expert

Chapter 14: What to Grow

You have your greenhouse built; you have containers, soil, and everything else you need to make your greenhouse successful, but where are your plants? With all the choices out there, it can be hard to decide what you want to grow. You need to remember to think about the temperature inside the greenhouse during the winter and how hot it is going to get during the summer.

The best vegetables to grow are the ones your family will eat, and that grow well indoors, like cucumbers, peas, beans, and greens. You can take advantage of plants that are cold-tolerant like greens in the winter months and plants that are heat-tolerant such as peppers in the summer.

The best vegetables would depend on your growing zone, the amount of space you have, and how cold or hot it gets inside your greenhouse. It is fun to grow some weird and interesting plants other than the tried and true plants, such as tomatoes.

Best Vegetables for a Greenhouse

It is exciting to think about all the plants that you can grow in your greenhouse. But there are times when it can be a bit overwhelming to decide between all the various plants and varieties.

Where should you start?

While you are thinking about which vegetables to grow in your greenhouse, you need to consider which ones grow best in a controlled environment. Keeping this in mind, you might want to choose between warm and cold season vegetables or those that love a certain setting like heat.

Below you will find a list of the best vegetables that are easy to grow inside a greenhouse.

Carrots

These are the most popular root crops that are very easy to plant. These can be planted during winter. You don't have to worry about them because they can handle the frost. If you worry about growing carrots, you can stop worrying. Just get some loose, sandy, well-tilled soil. This allows them to dive without being under any pressure. Make sure the soil isn't too thick, or you will have rounded dwarf carrots.

There haven't been any chemicals made that can keep away pests or diseases from carrots. Most varieties are already resistant to most diseases and pests. Just read the seed packets very carefully. Only sow seeds that are free of diseases. Working the soil regularly can overcome some of these obstacles. It is fine if you harvest them earlier than you expected. You can do this if you see any damage happening later during their maturity. Make sure you destroy any plants or residue that gets infected.

Carrots generally take between two and four months to ripen, and it all depends on the kind you are growing and the circumstances inside the greenhouse. Some kinds will require more weeks. They are usually ready in around 75 days. When you pull them, you might just end up with a handful of leaves. If this happens, just loosen the soil first before you try pulling them up.

- Well-tilled, sandy soil
- Choose disease-resistant
- Frost-resistant
- 75 days to harvest

Asparagus

If you are looking for a vegetable that will keep producing for 20 years, asparagus is the veggie for you. It is best planted from a one or two year crown. Twenty asparagus crowns can produce enough asparagus for a family of four.

Asparagus doesn't get along well with other plants. You need to get rid of any grasses or weeds around it. Don't ever plant another crop in the same place. The normal method of planting asparagus is by placing it in a trench. You need to plant it about 12 to 14 inches deep. Add lots of organic matter to the trench and mix it well. Set the crowns about a foot apart with the shoots aimed up. Make sure you leave some spears like the small ones. You could grow asparagus in containers if you would like.

Don't get too excited about the first harvest, and don't pick too much for a couple of years. They need to establish a stable root system to give them the energy they need. This will give you a good crop of spears next year.

- Plant alone
- Plant a foot apart
- Needs to establish for a couple of years before picking

Green Onions

Green onions grow fast in coastal, cooler climates or inside a greenhouse. These are the easiest crops to grow and are virtually maintenance-free. Onions are the most recommended beginner plants. They are best for beginning gardeners. You can begin the seedlings inside and transplant them outside if you would like.

You can either plant these from seeds or find onion sets. The best way to begin them is by planting sets. These are great as they thrive in every condition, and that includes inside greenhouses.

All you need to do is plant them in some well-drained soil and water them regularly when they are in the greenhouse. This needs to be done more often during the hot summer months. The best time to stop watering them is when they have swollen. Once the foliage turns yellow and begins dying back, you can harvest them. Now you need to dry them in the sun. It doesn't get any easier than that.

They resist diseases and pests; just make sure you sanitize your containers and flats with a ten percent bleach solution before you add the soil.

- Plant from sets
- Well-drained soil
- Water regularly
- Pick when foliage is yellow

Spinach

This is a cold, hardy leafy green. It is common and can be grown all year long. Most spinach will grow in cooler weather. Pests aren't usually a problem, especially for beginners.

They grow similar to lettuce, but spinach is more nutritious. You can eat it fresh or cooked. It has lots of vitamins, calcium, and iron than other vegetables.

Spinach loves either full sun or light shade as long as it is in soil that is drained well. Get the soil ready by adding in some manure about a week before you plant it. The soil's temperature shouldn't ever be more than 70 degrees. Seedlings are hard to transplant, which is why starting them inside isn't advised. Water them only when the soil gets dry. Once they germinate to a few inches, you can thin them out where they are three to four inches apart. You can use mulch to keep the soil moist.

You can harvest the leaves when they are large enough to eat. Harvest just the outer leaves. Let the ones in the center get larger. This allows the plant to grow. This will keep them from bolting.

- Cold, hardy
- Soil temperature – 70 degrees or below
- Water them sparingly

Tomatoes

It is very easy to grow tomatoes in a greenhouse. Nothing beats having a supply of tomatoes all year long. Try to find a variety that is resistant to diseases like verticillium and fusarium.

Tomatoes love the heat but can't stand cold weather. Inadequate light could make them frail and pale. There are many varieties to choose from, and picking the best ones can be hard. Think about the size of the tomato when it is full-grown.

Be sure to plant the seeds in soil that has good drainage. You need the soil moistened but not immersed with water. Make sure the temperature stays between 70 and 75 degrees. Put one seedling in each pot for healthy and strong plants. Don't hesitate to thin out the plants, since it needs to be done. Begin fertilizing when you see it produce the second set of leaves.

Tomatoes that you grow in a greenhouse are healthier for you as they will have a larger level of lycopene. This helps unclog your arteries. It is good for your heart.

- Temperature – 70 to 75 degrees
- Moist soil
- Does not like the frost

Cucumbers

Planting cucumbers might be a bumper crop for your greenhouse. Make sure you propagate your cucumbers in peat pots and not in flats. Their root systems can't get obstructed.
There are some ways that you can train the vines when you grow them in a greenhouse. There is the triple stem method. All suckers get taken off the developing creep up to the trellis. Another way is by lateral growth. Every sucker gets pinched off for the four to five fruit sets.

There are some diseases and pests that could harm the cucumber's growth. Spider mites are the worst. These are microscopic, but you will notice them by their webbing on the leaves and stems. You can spray them with insecticidal soap to reduce this population.

Cucumbers grow fairly fast. Don't let them get too big since it could cause them to taste bitter. Once they are ready to harvest, do so every few days. They will quit producing as they mature.

- Use peat pots, not flats
- Plant around the edges to train the veins
- Remove the suckers
- Watch out for spider mites

Best Herbs for a Greenhouse

Mint

Mint is invasive, but this makes it easy to grow. Mint carries runners underneath the soil so that it might appear in other parts of your growing area. They will compete with your other plants for nutrients, light, and water.

Plant them about two inches in the ground and a foot apart. Water them well. Measure the roots' capacity to reach other roots by using settling boards. You could place some bricks about a foot deep in the beds. You could place them in a large canister that you have sunken into the garden bed. You could use a container or pot and put it on a shelf.

If you notice any signs of mint rust, cut it off and throw it away. It could spread quickly to the soil and other plants. It could affect the new crops.

- Plant in containers
- Plant two inches in
- Plant two feet apart
- Water well

Cilantro

Cilantro grows best when planted in pots that have been filled with soil that drains well. It can grow to three feet tall and will self-seed.

This herb needs to be watered constantly. They will grow well in loose soil and full sun. They flower and go to seed in warm conditions. Don't transplant them as they have a long taproot that is very fragile. If you injure the taproot, it might not grow. The seeds will sprout when temperatures reach between 50 and 85 degrees. This will happen in about seven to ten days.

Get rid of any dead leaves and discard all debris. Wash off the leaves every now and then to disturb its normal spore-releasing cycle. Neem oil can be applied weekly to stop fungal invasions. Don't give it any unnecessary nitrogen.

Harvest the leaves as you need them. Cilantro is best when harvested early morning. Don't wash the leaves as they will lose their fragrant oils.

- Plant in containers
- Well-draining soil
- Lots of water and full sun
- Keep at 50 to 85 degrees

Sage

This can easily be grown from seeds. You can begin this perennial with other herbs like basil and rosemary. Once they are seedlings, you can transplant them about a foot apart.
Slugs and spider mites are the normal pests for sage. Some neem oil can keep these away. Get rid of any weeds and all other garden trash. Get rid of any plants that are too infested by putting them in the trash.

Delicately harvest leaves during its first year of growth. Pick as you need it during the year. Sage is best eaten fresh, but you can dry it and store it. Dried leaves will have a different taste that is very powerful than fresh leaves.

Dried sage is normally used in turkey stuffing. The seeds can be collected when the blooms turn brown and dry. Once it is completely dry, lightly crush the heads and get rid of the waste.

- Plant seedlings a foot apart
- Keep weeds and trash away
- Warm conditions, preferably over 70 degrees

Tarragon

Tarragon can be grown from seeds, cuttings, and seedlings. It is usually easier to plant about six seeds per pot in a moistened potting mix. They need to be grown in full sun and with plenty of airflow.

These herbs are hardy and can grow in sandy, dry, and poor soil. Tarragon has strong root systems, and this makes them very tolerant in desert-like conditions. They can survive for up to three years. They will eventually run out of steam and will need to be renewed.

There are two varieties of tarragon. French tarragon has a full flavor and is fancied by food enthusiasts. The Russian tarragon isn't as flavorful. Set your tarragon plants about 18 inches apart. You can eat both the leaves and flowers.

- Full sun
- Lots of airflow
- Sandy soil
- Little water

Basil

Basil is easy to care for plant that can easily be grown in a greenhouse. Basil likes being in well-drained, nutrient-rich soil. Basil will not tolerate a lot of water, so make sure wherever you have it planted, it has adequate drainage. It also likes the pH of the soil to stay around 6.0 and 7.5.

Basil will require at least six hours of sunlight. If you have a south-facing spot that gets six hours of sun, then that's where your basil needs to be. If you are using artificial lighting, the basil is going to need ten hours of light for healthy growth. However, you can use a combination of the two for the best results.

- Soil pH of 6.0 to 7.5
- Six hours of sunlight, at least
- Well-drained and nutrient-rich soil

Dill

Dill is another great culinary herb that is fairly easy to grow. It can easily be grown from seeds and is best grown that way as transplants don't always fare too well. Dill likes full sun, and other than that, it doesn't have many other requirements. It does well in poor and rich soil, and it doesn't mind if it is dry or wet.

- Any type of soil
- Full sun
- Regular watering

Best Fruits for a Greenhouse

Strawberries

This is the most common fruit grown in a greenhouse. Strawberries grown in a greenhouse will taste better than the ones you buy from grocery stores. Growing them inside a greenhouse will lessen any damage from disease and pests. You might want to bring some bumblebees into your greenhouse to pollinate your plants better. Just make sure you buy your seedlings from a reliable nursery and check them for diseases before you purchase them. Growing strawberries isn't difficult. You just need to follow the steps to grow them.

Place your strawberry plant in pots that have been packed with soil that is highly organic. The soil needs to drain well. You can use mulch to control the soil's temperature. You will need to use drip irrigation since they have such shallow roots.

Be sure your greenhouse stays clean at all times. Watch out for any indications of diseases and pests to keep any problems from getting worse. Strawberries are prone to verticillium wilt. You can keep this from happening by buying your plants from reputable sources. Don't plant them near tomatoes.

- Organic, well-drained soil
- Plant in pots
- Use drip irrigation for shallow roots
- Keep away from tomatoes

Cherries

Cherries can be planted in greenhouses. They don't take up that much space, and you can move them around. The species that don't have to be cross-pollinated are the easiest to grow.

They will fruit just like they will when grown outside as long as you have the correct combination of nutrients, water, temperature, and soil. Fertilize the tree once per year and make sure the greenhouse is ventilated well. Make sure the temperature inside the greenhouse doesn't rise too fast during the summer. Prune lightly with clean scissors. Get rid of any dead or broken branches. You can prevent diseases by making sure there is good airflow inside the greenhouse, keeping it pruned, and cleaning the greenhouse. Don't leave the aged fruit or leaves lying on the ground.

I know you might be excited to harvest the cherries, but you have to have patience. If you harvest them too soon, it could ruin the fruit. It could take up to three years to produce the right fruit.

- Fertilize once per year
- Lots of ventilation
- Steady temperature
- Regular watering, but not too much

Grapes

Grapes are not as demanding as vineyards may make them seem. All they require is some attention through watering, fertilizing, pruning, and training. It is easy to produce a stable crop for many years.

Start your plants from the opposite edge and move them in towards the door through training. Train them to climb the walls and roof and move closer to the door. You also have the option of starting the roots outside of the greenhouse and moving the plant inside. Make sure you water them every seven to ten days. They will need some pollination when the vine starts producing flowers. Get rid of curly tendrils.

- Plant along the edges
- Train up the walls of the greenhouse
- Remove curly tendrils
- Fertilize regularly

Lemons

Lemons are quite simple to grow, considering they need so little attention after they have been planted. It can easily thrive if you keep up with the ideal temperature, lighting, and moisture. The dwarf variety made for containers works best. This will give you the ability to move the plant to wherever it needs to be.

Lemon trees like it to be between 70 and 90 degrees. They also need at least eight hours of sun to grow, but if you can give them 12 hours, then they will grow even better. They have to have intense sunlight to induce flowers and to have the energy they need to create the fruit.

- Temperature – 70 to 90 degrees
- At least eight hours of sun, preferably 12
- Plant small varieties
- Plant in containers

Chapter 15: Plant Schedules

The goal of a greenhouse is to keep things growing year-round, right? How do you make sure you do that? You have to come up with a planting schedule, and for that, you have to take two things into consideration. One is the temperature, and the second is the day length.

Day length is likely the most important factor when it comes to determining when you should plant something in your greenhouse. If you don't plan on using supplemental lighting, it will be critical for you to know how long your days are for your area year-round. This is going to vary greatly depending on if you live in a Northern area or Southern area. It can also be affected by living in the mountains or the valleys. For the most part, February marks when the days and nights start to become equal, and the amount of sunlight during the day will start to grow from there until around November. Remember, though, this might not be true for you, especially if you live in New York, Oregon, Pennsylvania, and other similar states. Their days are still pretty short at that time. However, if you live in Nevada, Arizona, or certain parts of California, your days could be longer than your nights. Please, keep this in mind and come up with your own schedule based on your city. The planting schedule we will go over is an average, and you can adjust it to fit your local climate.

You also have to think about the temperature inside your greenhouse and the multiple microclimates within it, affecting plants' growth. The coldest areas of the greenhouse are normally close to the glazing and next to the vents. That's where you are going to want to plant your cold-hardy vegetables during the winter, such as kale and spinach. The warmest areas are normally along the north wall, where the sun reflects off and hits that area. When you plan out your planting schedule according to the length of the day, manage your plant's location based on temperature, and pick the right crops and varieties, you are going to be able to enjoy vegetables all year long.

Growing Guide and Planting Schedule

A planting schedule isn't just knowing what plants to plant when. It also involves the workings of the greenhouse. If you want to plant all year, maintenance goes into keeping your greenhouse running smoothly. In our planting schedule, which you can adjust to your needs, we will also go over important maintenance that you will need to keep up during the year.

- **January**

This is a pretty quiet time during the growing season. It provides you the best opportunity to give your greenhouse the once over and make sure that everything is functioning as it should, especially if your greenhouse is on the older side.

Make sure during this time that you keep your temperatures above 45, but you don't need to let the temperatures get higher than 60. Keep your plants well lit, but cover them up if there is a chance of frost. Water them according to their needs, and make sure you don't wet the plant or their staging so that they don't develop a disease. Keep an eye out for pests and slugs. This is also the time to order compost and seeds for the spring.

As for your plants, feed the spring-flowering bulbs, like narcissus, crocus, and hyacinth. Store polyanthus and pot-grown roses inside. This is the time to take cuttings from chrysanthemums. Put rooted seedlings, like pelargonium, in pots. You can sow some bedding plants in a heated propagator, such as carnations, verbena, and lobelia. You can early plant potatoes for cropping in May.
To keep the risk of disease down, keep the atmosphere dry and don't overwater your plants unless they are flowering. It is best to water early on and keep the water directed towards the roots. If water hits the floor, bench, or foliage, it can increase the humidity in the greenhouse and increase the risk of mold and pests.

- **February**

You will likely need to start watering more often; just make sure that the soil is not overwatered. Keep an eye on frosty weather and keep your temperature constant. You need to cover tender plants and spray for pests. This is also when you need to prepare seed trays. While the outside weather may be warming up, try to avoid exposing the plants to fluctuations in temperature and try to keep things around 42 to 60 degrees. All frost-sensitive plants need to be kept covered if you are struggling to keep the greenhouse temperature above 42.

You can start to sow more plants this month to get a good head start before spring. You will want to sow bedding plant seeds. You can bring your stored dahlia, hydrangea, and fuchsia into the sunlight. Sow your tomato seeds, as well as eggplants, peas, broad beans, cabbage, sprouts, parsnips, and onions. You can now place strawberry runners into pots.

- **March**

During this time, you need to make sure that the temperature stays between 45 and 65. This may be a good growing time, and when things get up and running, it can also present issues with fluctuating temperatures, depending on the area where you live. These fluctuations can cause problems, as a bright sunny day could cause your greenhouse to become overheated. Aim to keep the temperature around 45 to 65 degrees. Keep the greenhouse heated at night and ventilated during the day. For your young plants, use liquid fertilizer. This is when pests become a bigger issue. Keep an eye out for red spider mites, whiteflies, and greenflies, and spray if needed. If it would help your plants, you can use capillary matting. This is also when you should prepare hanging baskets.

Your bedding plant seedlings from last month should be planted, and you can sow plants that you want to grow later in the year right now. Seedlings need plenty of sun, but you will want to protect them from the hottest midday sun as they could easily be scorched. If you wish to, take cuttings from fuchsia and chrysanthemum. Prick out your tomato seedlings, and sow cucumber seeds. This is also a good time to plant peppers, leeks, runner beans, sweet corn, celery, and zucchini. You will also need to do some hand pollinating as pollinating insects are not yet active.

- **April**

Hopefully, this month will bring about warmer weather. Make sure the temperature of the greenhouse stays between 45 and 70. Open up the roof vents. On sunny days, use shading or newspaper to cover your seedlings. As always, keep an eye out for pests feeding on your growing plants. You can start using less heat at this time and getting rid of some insulation. Since it is getting warmer, your plants are going to get thirstier, and you will likely need to water them more often.

This is a good time to sow marigold seeds. Prick out any bedding plants that your started last month and harden them off. Plant your dahlia cuttings, along with sweet peas and pansies. Pick out the side shoots and feed your tomatoes. Move the cucumbers into a bigger, growing space. Sow zucchini and marrow for May or June plant outs. You can start to harvest some strawberries. You can split and re-pot certain houseplants.

- **May**

You will likely have a greenhouse full of vibrant, healthy plants this month, so you get to look forward to spending some extra time in there to stay on top of ventilation and watering. This also means you are moving away from keeping the greenhouse warm to keep the greenhouse cool.

When sunny, make sure the greenhouse temperature stays below 80. You can use shading, especially along the south-facing glass. You may still need some heating during the night. Open your ventilators if you have to, and open the door as well if need be. The is the slightest bit of chance in certain areas for frost at night, so keep an eye on the weather. Damp down floors if your weather is sunny to cool and humidify the greenhouse. Make sure you keep up with watering and feeding the plants.

Pot any of the cuttings that you have taken from plants that have developed roots. You can take cuttings from houseplants at this time. You can also harden off your bedding plants. Create your hanging baskets that will get placed out in June. Harden off your dahlia plants. Train your cucumber and tomato plants, and water and feed them. Continue to harvest some of the earlier planted strawberries, potatoes, French beans, and lettuce.

Plants are actively growing at this time, and tying and staking may need to be performed during this time. If you are not growing plants directly in the ground, you have to make sure that you feed them regularly because the plant's roots can seek out food from the earth. If you are looking to stimulate the growth of the leaves, you will need high-nitrogen feed and high-potassium feed when they are flowering or producing fruit.

- **June**

You should no longer need greenhouse heating. Service and store the heaters until the winter. Scorching is a bigger problem at this point. Some common signs of scorching are growth slowing down, flowers lacking color, and leaves showing scorch signs. Continue to use shading on plants that are prone to scorching. Keep the temperature down in the greenhouse by ventilating. Water and feed your plants regularly. Damp down the floors during sunny to cool weather and humidity. If you are keeping any type of outside garden, you can move those plants out of the greenhouse and harden them off for planting. Clean and tidy up your trays and pots.

Ensure that all dangers of frost have passed before you start moving any of your plants outside. Chrysanthemum and carnations can be moved outside. Hanging baskets can also be moved outside. Plant your summer flowering bedding plants in the garden. Harvest early cucumbers and tomatoes along with radishes, beetroot, French beans, carrots, and lettuce. Melons and cucumbers will also need to be trained.

As you move some of your plants outside, you can start to tidy up your greenhouse a bit. Make sure you don't leave dirty pots, dead leaves, or discarded plants lying around. These are perfect breeding grounds for disease and pests.

- **July**

As summer gets closer to its peak, the main problem in a greenhouse is making sure it doesn't get too hot. Ventilation is vital to ensure good air circulation. If the temperature is extremely hot, opening all of the vents and propping open the door may not be enough to keep things comfortable inside. You will likely need to use shades and damp down the greenhouse. These will help, but you may need to bring in an air circulating fan to force ventilation and make sure that the temperatures stay in the right range. Continue to use shading on plants prone to scorching.

The higher temperatures also mean your plants will dry out quicker, so water and regularly feed your plants. Continue to damp down the floors and humidify the greenhouse. You can also take cuttings.

Move pelargoniums and fuchsias outside. You can move container-grown roses outside. You can take cuttings from shrubs like weigela and forsythia. Continue to harvest tomatoes and cucumbers. You can also sow parsley. Peg down any strawberry runners you have. Harvest peppers, radishes, and lettuces.

You also have to stay on top of pests and diseases as they can easily overtake your plants if you aren't careful. At the first signs, you need to spray so that they don't take hold. You can also use those hanging sticky fly traps. They may not be pretty, but they can help to catch pests that fly before they have a chance of laying eggs. You may also want to install screens on your vents and doors to make sure that birds can't get inside.

- **August**

Keep an eye out for mold and use a fungicide if you need to be. If grey mold ends up affecting any flowers, fruit, or leaves, destroy the affected areas and spray with a fungicide. Regulate your heat with ventilators. Water and feed regularly. You can plant certain bulbs and take cuttings. This is when you should plant cyclamen, narcissus, and hyacinths for Christmas cuttings. You can take cuttings from pelargonium and fuchsia, as well as lavender and hebe cuttings. Continue to harvest peppers, radishes, lettuce, cucumbers, and tomatoes. Plant potatoes in pots for winter harvesting.

With salad crops and flowers at their peak, August is the best time to take stock and reflect on the successes from the season so far. Learn from any mistakes you may have made when it comes to creating your plans for next year. You can also store some seeds to use next year.

- **September**

Temperatures will often fluctuate at this time, and heaters might be needed. Get rid of shading for maximum lighting in the greenhouse. Move frost-sensitive plants inside of the greenhouse. Check your plants for pests before you take them into the greenhouse.

Make sure all of your potted plants are brought in before the first frost. Sow sweet peas and pansies for the spring. Store fuchsia and pelargonium plants. Continue to harvest eggplants, peppers, and tomatoes. You should clean up your cucumber plants as they should no longer be producing.

- **October**

Make sure you keep the greenhouse above 45. Ventilate only on days that are warm. Water plants carefully and sparingly. Get rid of deadheads, fallen leaves, and so on to prevent mold. Take all of your half-hardy plants inside. Insulate your greenhouse if you need to.

Plant snowdrop, crocus, hyacinth, and tulip bulbs for the spring. Move the chrysanthemums into the greenhouse and cut flowers. Remove the tomato plants once they are finished producing. Harvest the last of the tomatoes, eggplants, and peppers. You can also sow spring cropping lettuces.

- **November and December**

You should think about removing shading and cleaning the glass, framework, and staging with garden-safe disinfectant during this time. This is also the best time to go through and repair any cracks or holes that could cause you to lose heating. During this, you should insulate the greenhouse and make sure any downpipes or gutters aren't blocked with leaves. Ensure that the greenhouse is cool and dry and ventilated on sunny days. Your heaters will need to be working properly. Also, go through and clean and tidy your flower pots, trays, and so on, and store them neatly so that they are ready for spring.

For your plants, make sure that hydrangeas and fuchsias are stored under staging during the winter. Dahlia and chrysanthemum tubers need to be stored. You can plant your iris bulbs for the spring. Get annuals like pansies and sweet peas ready for bedding in the spring, and pot perennials like delphinium and lupins. You can also sow types of French beans, carrots, and lettuce. You can also move mint, parsley, and chives into pots to keep a winter supply.

Chapter 16: Caring for Your Plants

A big part of keeping up your greenhouse is going to be caring for your plants. There are many different aspects that are a part of caring for your plants. The things we will be going over in this chapter may not apply to every plant you grow, but many will. Our first logical stop is going to be starting your seeds.

Starting Seeds

Before you can grow anything, you have to make sure that the seeds germinate. Here's a good way to start your seeds to ensure they grow the best they can. Start by filling seed-starting trays, flowerpots, or peat pots with moist seed-starting mix. Then add the seeds in, planting them according to the directions on their packet. Usually, you will plant two or three seeds per pot at a depth of an eighth to a half-inch. Cover the seeds with soil and then mist it with some water.

Cover the trays or pots with plastic wrap, and then place them in a warm, brightly lit location. You can use a heating mat made for seed starting, which will allow you to regulate the temperature of the soil. Once the seedlings start to appear, take off the plastic wrap.

Make sure that you keep the planting mix moist but not waterlogged. Snip off any excess seedlings with some scissors. You only need one seedling per pot. Fertilize the seedlings every one to two weeks with a 5-10-5 water-soluble fertilizer.

When the seedlings are about eight weeks old, you can harden them off and plant them where you want.

Pollination

Pollination is what causes the formation of seeds and fruit. Wind, butterflies, bees, and birds are natural pollinators. A greenhouse forms a barrier that protects plants from adverse conditions, but it also creates an obstacle for pollination. There will have to be a bit of human intervention to ensure that plants are successfully pollinated.

With a small greenhouse, you can try manual pollination. Manually pollinating is cost-effective and only takes some time. All you have to do is gently shake plants or tap flowers to release pollen from the male flower to the female flower. Like squash, some plants have female and male flowers, so you will have to pollinate by move pollen from a male flower to the female flower. Others, like tomatoes, have "perfect flowers," meaning they contain male and female parts. Disturbing the flowers on these plants will help to distribute the pollen to where they need to go.

There is also a device pollination. It is a battery-operated tool that greenhouse supply companies carry. It is a hand-held pollinator want that has a vibrating head that you touch to the base of the flower. Alternatively, you can use an electric toothbrush to pollinate flowers. Whether you choose a device or manual pollination, you need to make sure you pollinate your plants between ten AM and three PM.

Another option is bee pollination. Bumblebees are more effective than other types of bees because they have longer tongues and wing vibrations. There are some species of bumblebees that are raised for use in greenhouses. You can buy a hive or box of bees and place it inside of your greenhouse. You will provide them with a supplemental food source, like nectar, to make sure that they survive. Since the greenhouse is a closed environment, you need to make sure you don't use pesticides that could kill your bees.

Crop Steering

Crop steering is a way to manage plant growth by changing the climate and irrigation to force a certain response from a plant.

When you change the environmental condition, growers can steer the growth of a plant towards generative or vegetative. You can crop steer at every stage of growth, include with propagation, plants, and more.

Vegetative growth is when the leaves and stems are growing, and generative is when it starts producing flowers and fruits.

You can achieve crop steering through irrigation. The timing, amount, and frequency of irrigation will influence the plant's response and will push their growth towards a certain stage. Adjusting your irrigation specifically for the stage of development, genetics, and environment, will lead to an improved final product. If you would like the plant to grow faster, you can use vegetative irrigation like this:

- Using small shot sizes often in irrigation, lower EC at the dripper and in the roots, and keeping the roots at a higher temperature
- Having dry backs between irrigations and overnight
- Keeping a higher WC at the roots

If you want to steer it towards generative, you will do the opposite of those steps. These will help the plants to recover and grow faster while keeping their vigor.

You can also steer with climate. For some, you can switch the day-night cycle to 12 hours on and 12 off, and this can induce flowers. Like a change with the photoperiod, other climate factors can help to steer the plants' growth from vegetative to generative. If you have higher temperatures, your plants will be steered more towards vegetative.

Pruning and Trellising

There are many plants that will require pruning and trellising, and tomatoes are important for these practices to ensure good yields. Trellising the vines, and pruning suckers and lower leaves, improves air circulation, balances vegetative and reproductive growth, supports the weight of the fruits and plants, and maintains overall good hygiene. Keeping your fruit off the soil will make it easier to pick and decreases the number of blemishes.

Creating the trellis is an important part of the process. You will have to suspend strings from a support system of wires that are at a height of at least seven feet. It is best to set up the trellis before planting so that you don't disturb the plants once they have gotten established.

If the frame of your greenhouse can support a mature crop's weight, you can attach the wire right to the purlins of the greenhouse. This typically gives you the most vertical space. However, the bearing load on the wire will be around 15 pounds per foot. If you don't want to use the frame, you will need to place tall posts at the ends of the rows and possible throughout the row, and attach the wire to those.

Make sure that the posts can accommodate the plant's height and 18 additional inches that will be driven into the ground. Drive your posts 18 inches into the ground and keep them no more than 20 feet apart. The end posts should be strengthened further by anchoring them with a wire or another stake. Stretch the wires tightly between the opposite ends of the support structure and secure them. You will need to have one wire for each row of tomatoes.

After you have planted the crop, loosely tie the string or twine around the base of your plant. If the knot ends up becoming too tight, it can cut into the plant as it grows larger. You can also use tomato trellis clips that encircle the stem and clamp onto the string. You will have to add another clip to the stem at every 12 inches as the plant grows.

Then you will need to keep up with pruning. To balance the vegetative and reproductive growth for large-fruited crops, you should prune to only one or two leaders. For smaller fruit plants, like grape or cherry tomatoes, you can have four leaders. Limiting your suckers and leaders gives the plant the chance to focus their energy on developing their fruit instead of maintaining the shoots, causing smaller fruit.

You can start pruning suckers once the first flower cluster has developed, and you should continue to do this throughout the crop's life. Make sure you prune with the foliage is dry and make sure your tools and hands are sanitized before and after your prune them. The easiest way to get rid of the sucker is by hand while they are small. Suckers are small offshoots that form at the V between the stalk and branch of the plant.
You can also go through and prune the leaves on the lower part of the plants to help push the plant's energy up for fruit production. It also helps with air flowers. Once your plant has around 18 to 20 leaves, start removing one to three leaves each week with sterilized pruners.

Fertilizing

All plants will need some sort of fertilizer. Let's go through some of the things you need to consider when fertilizing. The first thing to consider is the substrate. If you are using some like perlite or rock wool, they provide little to no nutrients. However, if you are using organic substrate components like peat moss, they are going to have some nutrients that your plants can use. In this same category is compost. If you wanted to use mulch or bark, they have to be completely composted before you use it or continue to compost and rob the nitrogen plant.

You will also need to know what is in your water. Water can contain things like magnesium and calcium, and its pH can also affect the plants. If the water you are using was filtered through reverse osmosis, then fertilizers are more important.
Plants won't need fertilizer until a week after germination. They only need a small amount of nitrogen, potassium, and phosphorus. Remember, plants aren't going to grow faster just because you add more fertilizer. In fact, you can burn them.

When you are preparing your fertilizer, you will want to keep two different solutions. One will contain iron, nitrogen, and calcium. The second will have sulfate, phosphorus, magnesium, potassium, and micronutrients. You do not want to mix phosphate and calcium because they do not mix well. You want your fertilizer to be soluble, and certain mixtures won't be soluble in the water. If you don't feel comfortable mixing your own fertilizer, please feel free to purchase store-bought mixtures. They are just as good and can make a beginner's job a lot easier.

You have to be careful with calcium as the uptake is highly dependent on plant transpiration. If the uptake is low because of slow transpiration during cold or cloudy weather or hot and dry weather, the plant won't be able to get the water it needs, and this can cause a deficiency in calcium. This can end up causing blossom end rot.

Pests

You may have a greenhouse, but pests will still find a way inside. Pest management is vital to keeping the plants happy and healthy. Common pests are whiteflies, mites, aphids, mealybugs, thrips, fungus gnats, slugs, and caterpillars. The crazy thing about pests is that most of them are so small they are hard to spot. Many times, they have already caused a lot of damage before you notice them. Luckily, you can prevent these problems through preventative care.

You can use sticky cards placed near sensitive plants to keep an eye on any possible pest problems. They should be replaced weekly during the summer pest season. There are several pests that can be killed with insecticidal soaps; these include thrips, whiteflies, mites, mealybugs, and aphids. All you have to do is liberally spray the plant with insecticidal soap once a week.

Other pests will need stronger methods, so that you could try neem oil. All you have to do is cover them plant with the neem oil, normally mixed with water, and repeat once a week. You can also use your fingernail or thin-bladed knife to lift the protective coverings to spot check for the dead bugs.

You can use Bacillus Thuringiensis in the soil to get rid of tiny flies. Slugs and caterpillars are best hand-picked and tossed into a bucket of soapy water. Make sure you check the plants, undersides of benches, and any debris to see if there are any hiding in those spaces. Slugs and caterpillars are probably the most dangerous pests.

Chapter 17: Dealing With the Seasons

With the changing of the seasons, environmental concerns for growers will change as well. Even when you have a greenhouse, where you do have control over your surroundings, changes in the weather can greatly impact the growing process.

A greenhouse is nothing more than a mini-ecosystem that captures the growing forces of nature, holds them within an artificial bubble, and mimics the natural effects of air movement, humidity, heat, water, nutrients, and sunlight.

The nature of a greenhouse is to modify the climate to help expand the growing season. Decorative flowers and edible plants can be seeded a lot earlier in a greenhouse than outdoors. This gives you the chance to continually harvest in a year-round greenhouse, which will yield more crops than if they left for nature to mature.

Year-Round Growing

Keeping up a year-round greenhouse has become more popular in cooler North American climates. This is all thanks to advancements in technology, evolving plant species, and more accessible horticultural knowledge. Today, many commercial and home gardeners operate a year-round greenhouse that provides them with nearly as much produce during the cold winter months as in the humid and hot summertime.

With the right combination of winter greenhouse plants and the right climate control, you can have a successful winter growing season. Late fall to early spring used to be the time when green thumbs would wait for the snow and ice to leave while they pass their time looking through seed catalogs and planning out their plantings.

Now, growing things in a greenhouse during the winter has become a popular way to create more production options and enjoy the great-tasting crops that don't require a bunch of weeding, pest control, and watering. Planning out your crop plantings is important for optimal harvesting and is important for greenhouse gardening in the winter.

Cold season growing is slower to get started and has a later return than warm weather gardening, and this takes special knowledge on which crops you should and plant and what conditions they are going to need in order to survive.

While winter greenhouse gardening will take longer to have results, there is a huge trade-off in that they will stay fresher for longer than vegetables raised during the hot summer days.
Successful winter growing in a greenhouse is going to require a basic understanding of the science involved in the climate control and construction of the greenhouse, as well as a solid understanding of the right types of winter-hardy plants that will thrive during the winter. As the weather outside changes, you will have to face changes inside of your greenhouse as well.

Changes In Lighting
It's important that you are aware of the higher levels of light at different points of the year. Having an irrigation system can help out with certain nutritional issues that could be caused by changes in light. As the amount of light increases during the spring and summer, the need for nutrients and water rise, and these needs decrease during the fall and winter. That's why an irrigation system can help make things easier.

Rising Humidity
Higher humidity levels are more of an issue for older plants later in the year than they are for newly planted crops. During the spring, air temperatures tend to be cooler, so things tend to be too dry in the greenhouse. That's why it's important to artificially raise humidity levels in your greenhouse until the temperature outside naturally goes up. This can help prevent

crops from getting hit by increase light levels and dry conditions, which can be very stressful to your plants.

Then as the temperatures rise outside, there is going to be more humidity in your greenhouse. Signs that you have too much humidity in your greenhouse would cause condensation on the walls, which can drip on your plants and make them susceptible to fungal pathogens. You can also experience issues with pollination when humidity is high.

To help battle the high humidity levels, try dipping the temperatures in the evening by bringing in cold air. This will halt transpiration. If it is done right, this can keep condensation from forming the next day.

Winter Greenhouse Gardening
Growing in a greenhouse during the winter is going to have two main differences from summertime growing. First is the amount of natural sunlight you will have available, especially in the northern latitudes. Second is the ambient or existing natural outdoor temperature.

You can easily overcome these issues through artificial lights in the proper ultraviolet scale, which will replace the sunlight and add artificial heat to keep the temperature at the right levels. This will help to replicate the ideal summer conditions.

But the expense that comes with these processes defeats the purpose of working with nature and to make winter conditions to work for you. This means you would choose plants that are better suited to the shorter days. If you try to replicate summer weather, it will cause higher utility costs, and any cost savings realized by growing your own food in the winter will become moot after you factor in the extra costs.

Working with nature, and not against it, is the main philosophy of greenhouse winter gardening. When it comes to planting in the winter, choosing crops that respond to lower light levels and shorter days are important. It's just as important to choose crops that withstand greater fluctuations of humidity.

A lot of these conditions can be controlled. Once you have picked out the right plants and planted them in the proper seasonal rotation periods, the steps to take to have a successful winter garden focus on controlling the climate in the greenhouse to maintain the weather that cold-weather crops prefer. The first thing is to understand how cold-climate crops respond to the conditions you control in your greenhouse.

How to Achieve Optimal Conditions

The science of plants is rather straightforward. Plants use photosynthesis to change sunlight into energy. They consume carbon dioxide and release oxygen. Plants also have to have hydration through water that will supply them with nutrients. The water is moved through the root system, and any excess water is discharged through transpiration, where the plant will evaporate moisture through their leaves. This is a critical part of plant health, and it's important to manage this process in a greenhouse setting.

Too much humidity is just as bad as keeping your plants too dry. Plants that are unable to transpire excess water can rot. Every type of plant is going to have their own needs, but in general, plants that do well during the winter depend more on being in the right humidity levels and temperature than having a lengthy amount of time in the sun. The proper balance of humidity, air movement, ventilation, temperature, nutrients, water, and light presents a challenge for winter gardening.

There is an entire branch of science dedicated to winter gardening. It begins with figuring out how temperature, humidity, and ventilation affect different plants suitable for growing in your winter greenhouse.

After figuring out what plants do well in a winter greenhouse, you have to control the humidity through ventilation and temperature to make sure your plants go well. In most greenhouses, existing or ambient air temperature is determined through the outside conditions, artificial heat source, and greenhouse design. Winter-hardy plants can survive in cold air temperatures as long as the roots can't freeze. Plant leaves can withstand short-term cool temperatures, but they are very susceptible to excess water.

High humidity is one of the biggest threats to winter plant survival, and it's cold temperatures where the relative humidity becomes the most dangerous to the health of a plant. High humidity in cold temperatures can cause condensation to form on plants. Liquid water will allow the plant to freeze more easily and adds to a greater risk of fungal pathogen pollutants, like powdery mildew, mold, and spores.

Fortunately, it is easy to control relative humidity by reducing the amount of excess water you have in the greenhouse and increase the airflow and ventilation. They are all intrinsically connected.

Relative Humidity
The relative humidity is often misunderstood. RH is basically the ratio between the total water-holding capacity and the weight of water present in the air at a certain pressure and temperature. Air temperature is one of the biggest factors in figuring out how much moisture air can hold before it becomes super-saturated and gives off excessive water, typically as condensation. The pressure is secondary.

Warm air will hold more moisture than cold, just like high-pressure holds more moisture than low-pressure. The actual amount of water in the air is relative to how much moisture the air can hold at a certain temperature and pressure.

Chapter 18: Flowers and Ornamentals

You aren't limited to only fruits and vegetables in your greenhouse. You can also grow many gorgeous flowers and ornamental plants in your greenhouse. A greenhouse gives you the chance to enjoy seeing pretty blooming plants all year long. With solar heating and lighting, you can maintain some of the most exciting flowers that you can find, and in most cases, ensures that your garden always has some type of color. You must understand that you keep the temperature and water in your greenhouse regulated to make sure that your plants are able to thrive.

Flowers that are grown in a greenhouse often grow taller, bloom earlier, and don't have as many imperfections thanks to the protective nature of a greenhouse. Bulbs will normally do well in the winter and yield blooms by February.

Let's go over some of the best flowers to grow in a greenhouse.

Amaryllis
This is a tropical flower and is one of the easiest of all flowering bulbs to grow. You can find these in solid colors, like orange, salmon, pink, white, and red, as well as multicolored and striped varieties.

Amazon Lilies
The Amazon Lily can reach upwards of two feet in height and has a beautiful white blossom that is fragrant and keeps your greenhouse smelling sweet. It is grown from a bulb and is tropical by nature, which means that it is going to need to be in at least a 70-degree environment so that it doesn't die. In addition to this, you will find that Amazon lilies do better when grown in containers.

You can also grow many other lily species if you want. Just make sure that you don't overwater them and that they get at least eight hours of light each day. Try to make sure that most of these eight hours are natural sunlight, but you can supplement with artificial lighting as well.

African Violets

If you want a flower that offers you a spray of colors, African violets may be what you are looking for. You need to make sure that you use only low nutrient soil and have high humidity levels. This will give you the best possible result. It would be a good idea to get a growing bench and then let the violets have an area to thrive and grow when possible. Make sure that you don't get the leaves wet as it can change the way they look.

One trick that you may want to try out when you get a plant you really like is to take some leaf cuttings as a way to create a brand new plant. Unlike many other flowers, these plants are reproduced in this many, instead of a seed that undergoes a gestation period.

Chenille Plants

While some people may want actual flowers, other people may prefer shrubs or bushes in the greenhouse. One option would be chenille plants. This beautiful bush can reach six feet tall and have long, bright red cattail flowers.

Chinese Hibiscus

While a hibiscus can have a gorgeous appearance, you have to make sure that you are doing everything that you can to maintain a constant temperature within the greenhouse. The reason for this is that a sudden drop in temperature can cause them to die. The Chinese hibiscus can be found in a variety of different colors like white, pink, red, yellow, and more. Their blooms can reach up to four inches across and will make your greenhouse prettier. The flowers on the plant only last 24 hours before they wilt and die. Using nutrient-rich soil will help to give you the best possible blossoms and make sure that you keep the flower watered.

Christmas Cactus
This is an often-overlooked holiday bloom. While it does need water, it doesn't need as much during the winter and even less after its flowering despite its cactus name. A Christmas cactus has to have a balance of light, but less light if you would like it to have more blooms.

Impatiens
You can find these flowers in white, pink, peach, purple, orange, and red. They do very well in a greenhouse when you have a temperature of around 70 degrees. They are susceptible to cold, and their seeds will need ten to 14 days to germinate.

Pansy
The rich purples, reds, yellows, and blues of pansies will thrive in the cooler winter temperatures, both withstanding and performing better when the temperatures are on the lower side. When they grow in temperatures between 50 and 60, they will be hardier and have thick, dark leaves.

Roses
Roses are likely one of the most popular flowers grown in a greenhouse. They are typically grown in a greenhouse because they don't do very well in colder weather. Rose farmers house their plants in units that hold a steady temperature of anywhere from 70 to 80 degrees.

Keep in mind, though, that a full day of sunlight is needed for the plants to grow to the best of their ability. You will also find that roses come in many different styles, and each has its own planting needs. A good idea is to speak with your local nursery to make sure that you know what you will need to do to keep your flowers happy and healthy. You will also need to make sure you have special food for roses.

Snapdragon
The tall, pretty blooms of the snapdragon will add a touch of spring to your greenhouse, and you can even cut the flowers and bring a bouquet of them into your home. They like

temperatures between the mid-60s to low 70s, with more light as they grow bigger to help encourage flowers' production.

Orchids
Orchids are one of the most sensitive flowers out there. They can't deal with weather that is too cold, and they will die quickly in weather that is moderately warmer. This is why they are most often grown in greenhouses. This is because the temperature requirements can be maintained, and they will still get enough light to survive.

For orchids, you are going to have to make sure that you keep them at no less than 70 degrees, with a max temperature of 80 degrees. At night, you are going to want to make sure that you drop the temperature between 50 and 60 degrees to keep them stimulated.
When you do this, you can successfully grow an orchid and keep the flower growing strong. They also tend to do better in humid conditions, so you will want to keep this in mind.

When you have a greenhouse, it is never too early to start dreaming of spring. You have the ability to enjoy the year-round joys of gardening beautiful flowers.

Chapter 19: How Greenhouses Affect Life

All throughout history, people have added greenhouses to their homes, schools, botanical centers, and health facilities to bridge the gap between indoor and outdoor space. These additions are typically rooms or buildings encased in glass or plastic. While some add value and style to properties, the decorative structures also come with many health benefits.

Doctors tell us that it is important that we all get between ten to 15 minutes of sunlight each day. This helps to lower the risk of many different diseases and increases our overall health. So when you are working in a garden, even if you're in a greenhouse, you are reaping the benefits of all of that sunlight. The following are just some of the benefits of keeping a greenhouse.

Vitamin D Creation
Some greenhouses are known as conservatories, and they often get used as sunrooms. Even if you don't have a conservatory and you have a simple greenhouse, being in them still means you are receiving sunlight. Sunlight is the best source of keeping your vitamin D levels in a healthy range. Healthy levels of vitamin D helps to prevent bone density loss, cancer, muscle weakness, and other health problems.

Blood Pressure
Everybody has something called nitric oxide in the blood and skin. Nitric oxide reacts to sunlight and will widen the blood vessels. Therefore, getting regular exposure to the sun can lower your blood pressure, which will lower your risk of strokes and heart attacks.

Mental Health
Have you ever noticed how you are happier in the summer and spring than you are in the winter? This is a very common occurrence and is known as Seasonal Affective Disorder.

Doctors think that sunlight is able to increase how much serotonin the brain produces. Serotonin is a hormone that makes us feel happy. With shorter days during the winter, paired with being inside more because of the cold weather, can cause our serotonin levels to drop. This can mean that we feel less happy. With a greenhouse, you can get sunlight and warmth all year round.

Overexposure to The Sun
We all know that sitting out in the direct sun for too long without proper protection can lead to issues like skin cancer. Using a greenhouse can help combat the dangers of overexposure to the sun. The plastic or glass that greenhouses are made from will help prevent the harmful UV rays from seeping inside. The rays are filtered through so that they become less harmful. That means you can enjoy a beautiful and sunny area without fearing overexposure.

Prevention of Strokes and Improve Cardiovascular Health
Doctors recommend that the average adult get two to three hours of moderately intense exercise each week, and gardening is a low-impact, enjoyable way of getting that exercise in. It doesn't require you to spend hours in the gym or running on the treadmill. A 2013 Swedish study showed that people over the age of 60 who maintained a garden reduced their risk of strokes and heart attacks by 27% and lowered their risk of death from all causes by 30%.

Gardening is a safe form of exercise for the older generation and those who have joint pain or reduce mobility. That doesn't mean it's not also a great form of exercise for everybody else as well.

Brain Health
One study performed on 3000 seniors found that gardening could reduce dementia by over 35%, with other studies finding similar results. Much like the cause of Alzheimer's disease, the reason why gardening can help with mental health is poorly

understood. However, some scientists have hazard guess that the physical demands of gardening combined with problem-solving, learning, and practical thinking work together to keep the brain and other cognitive functions active long into your retirement years.

Gardening isn't just a good way to prevent brain health problems. It can actually create a between the quality of life for those who already have Alzheimer's. A famous example of this is "Clive West's award-winning garden at Chelsea in 2008," which had been deliberately laid out to help relax and stimulate people with dementia and Alzheimer's. There are a lot of care facilities that actively encourage residents with degenerative brain diseases to actively maintain their own gardens.

Stress Relief
Stress is a major issue for pretty much everybody, and it can lead to many other issues. Stress causes the body to release cortisol. High levels of cortisol can lead to things like erectile dysfunction, disrupted menstrual cycles, gastrointestinal issues, joint disease, high blood pressure, heart disease, weight gain, and decreased immune function, among other things.

Gardening can help combat the effects of stress in two ways. One is by making a person more active, and, two, by giving people a feeling of accomplishment and satisfaction of a job well done. Gardening will lower your cortisol levels. Spending only a couple of hours in the garden every week can lower your cortisol levels dramatically.

Strengthened Immune System
As we've mentioned already, gardening is a great way to get vitamin D. However, vitamin D is not an essential vitamin for cardiovascular and heart health, but it is important in strengthening your immune system. It can lower the number of colds you suffer from.

Besides having a natural boost in your immunity from being in the sun, getting your hands in the dirt will give your immune system a boost. Mycobacterium Vaccae is a strain of bacteria from nearly all garden dirt. It is known as "friendly bacteria" as it can help reduce allergic reactions, several skin problems, diseases, and asthma.

Another bonus to gardening is that food preparation methods kill many of these friendly bacteria and industrial farming, which means when you eat your own home-grown produce, you take in more of the helpful bacteria and many other micronutrients.

Chapter 20: Is a Greenhouse Business Really Profitable

Since everybody seems to be taking their produce growing into their own hands, is running a greenhouse business still profitable in this day and age? Farmlands seem to disappear, and many urban and suburban farmers turn to high-density CEA techniques to create greenhouse businesses.

Many of these greenhouses cost about $35,000 to build, and that includes the cost to install electric and water lines. These greenhouses are often used to add a business line to an existing property or even for first-time farmers. Since it's on the small side, it can be operated in about 20 hours each week.

While all of this sounds good in theory, can it make any money? Yes, it is possible for a greenhouse to make money, but it is trickier than just a yes or no answer. One thing you have to consider is the type of plant that is grown. For example, tomatoes do fairly well in the greenhouse world. A greenhouse that can hold 700 plants can make $15,000 to $20,000 each year.

The cost to produce each plant is about $15 a year. Half of that is labor, and 25% is energy. If the growers do a lot of the work on their own, then it will save them some money. If they wanted to produce year-round, they are going to have the added cost of heating the greenhouse.

There are seven crops that do well in a greenhouse for making profits. Those include strawberries, herbs, spinach, cucumbers, peppers, lettuce, and tomatoes.

If you wanted to have a greenhouse business, it could be profitable if you make the right decisions. A small scale greenhouse is not going to make as much as a larger scale greenhouse either. These are all important things to consider if a greenhouse business is something you are thinking about doing.

Keep in mind, just because the business can be profitable does not mean you will be making six figures. In fact, a lot of greenhouse businesses make under $50,000 a year.

Conclusion

Thank you for making it through to the end of the book; let's hope it was informative and able to provide you with all of the tools you need to achieve your goals, whatever they may be.

The next step is to decide on what kind of greenhouse will fit your needs and start gathering the materials you need to create your greenhouse. There are a lot of options out there, so make sure you choose wisely. There are also several different ways to build a greenhouse. You can buy everything yourself, or you can order a kit, so weigh the options and the cost and choose what works best for you.

Having a greenhouse can be fun and fulfilling work. You also have the added advantage of having delicious produce all year round, so go get started.

Congratulations!

Now you know everything about Greenhouses

If you loved reading this book, please let me know your thoughts by leaving a review on Amazon, I would really appreciate that

Thank you!